WRIGHT FAMILY CENSUS RECORDS

1810-1900

FRANKLIN COUNTY
VIRGINIA

Robert N. Grant

HERITAGE BOOKS

2008

HERITAGE BOOKS

AN IMPRINT OF HERITAGE BOOKS, INC.

Books, CDs, and more—Worldwide

For our listing of thousands of titles see our website
at
www.HeritageBooks.com

Published 2008 by
HERITAGE BOOKS, INC.
Publishing Division
100 Railroad Ave. #104
Westminster, Maryland 21157

International Standard Book Numbers
Paperbound: 978-0-7884-2069-6
Clothbound: 978-0-7884-7218-3

Introduction To Appendix: Census Records, Franklin County, Virginia

This document is an appendix to a larger work titled Sorting Some Of The Wrights Of Southern Virginia. The work is divided into parts for each family of Wrights that has been researched. Each part is divided into two sections; the first section is text discussing the family and the evidence supporting the relationships and the second section is a descendants chart summarizing the relationships and information known about each individual.

The appendices to the work (of which this document is one) present source records for persons named Wright by county and by type of record with the identification of the person named and their Wright ancestors to the extent known.

The sources for the records listed in this appendix are the following:

1) 1810 through 1900 Censuses, Franklin County, Virginia, microfilm copies available at the National Archives, Pacific Sierra Division, 1000 Commodore Drive, San Bruno, California 94066.

2) 1850 Census, Franklin County, Virginia, transcribed copy by Marvin U. Neighbors, 1975.

3) 1860 Census for Franklin County, Virginia, abstracted by Mrs. Iva J. Cook, Route 5, Box 630, Rocky Mount, Virginia 24151.

4) Franklin County, Virginia 1850 & 1860 Censuses, compiled by Karen Mann Robuck, Gateway Press, Inc., 1001 N. Calvert Street, Baltimore, Maryland 21202, 1990.

5) The 1870 Census Of Franklin County, Virginia, transcribed by Henry Hopkins & Beverly Merritt, H&M Publishing, P.O. Box 316, Ferrum, Virginia 24088, January 20, 2001.

6) 1880 Census for Franklin County, Virginia, abstracted by Mrs. Iva J. Cook, Route 5, Box 630, Rocky Mount, Virginia 24151.

7) The 1880 Census Of Franklin County, Virginia, transcribed by Henry Hopkins & Beverly Merritt, H&M Publishing, P.O. Box 316, Ferrum, Virginia 24088, January 20, 2001.

The identification of a person or their ancestor by year and county indicates their year of death and county of residence at death. For example, "1763 Thomas Wright of Bedford County" indicates that this was the Thomas Wright who died in 1763 in Bedford County. If no state is listed after the county, the state is Virginia; counties in states other than Virginia will have a state listed after the county, as in "1876 William S. Wright of Highland County, Ohio".

A parenthetical after the name indicates an identification of the person when a place of death is not yet known, as in "John Wright (Goochland County Carpenter)". A county in parentheses after the name indicates the county with which that person was most identified when no evidence of the place of death has yet been found, as in "Grief Wright (Bedford County)".

0304(102201)

All or portions of the text and descendants charts for each Wright family identified are available from the author:

Robert N. Grant
15 Campo Bello Court   (H) 650-854-0895
Menlo Park, California 94025   (O) 650-614-3800

This is a work in process and I would be most interested in receiving additional information about any of the persons identified in these records in order to correct any errors or expand on the information given.

WRIGHT FAMILY

CENSUS RECORDS

FRANKLIN COUNTY, VIRGINIA

1810 TO 1900

Revised as of October 22, 2001

TABLE OF CONTENTS

FRANKLIN COUNTY, VIRGINIA

1810 CENSUS

FRANKLIN COUNTY, VIRGINIA

Appendix: Franklin County, Virginia, 1810 Census:

Name of Town, city or County	Names of Heads of families	Free White Males					Free White Females				
		Under ten years of age to 10	Of ten years, and under sixteen to 16	Of sixteen, and under twenty-six including heads of families to 26	Of twenty-six and under forty-five including heads of families to 45	Of forty five and upwards, including heads of families 45&c	Under ten years of age to 10	Of ten years, and under sixteen to 16	Of sixteen, and under twenty six including heads of families to 26	Of twenty-six and under forty five, including heads of families to 45	Of forty-five and upwards, including heads of families 45&c
	William Wright	1	1	1	1	0	2	1	0	1	0
	Thomas Wright	2	1	0	0	1	0	1	3	0	1
	Joseph Wright	0	0	0	2	0	1	0	1	0	0
	Joseph Wright Sr.	0	1	3	1	0	1	0	0	1	0
	Wright Wright	1	0	1	1	0	0	0	1	0	00
	William Wright	0	0	2	1	1	0	1	2	1	1
	Hyrum Wright	0	0	1	0	0	1	0	1	0	0
	John Wright	3	0	2	1	0	1	1	1	0	00
	George Wright	2	3	0	0	1	4	4	1	1	0

Appendix: Franklin County, Virginia, 1810 Census:

Names of Heads of families [continued from prior page]	All other free persons except Indians, not taxed	Slaves	Identification
William Wright	0	5	1854 William Wright of Campbell County, son of 1814 John Wright of Bedford County and grandson of John Wright (Goochland County Carpenter)
Thomas Wright	0	0	1849 Thomas Wright of Franklin County, son of 1815 Joseph Wright of Bedford County and grandson of 1763 Thomas Wright of Bedford County
Joseph Wright	0	0	1829 Joseph F. Wright of Missouri, son of 1849 Thomas Wright of Franklin County, grandson of 1815 Joseph Wright of Bedford County, and great grandson of 1763 Thomas Wright of Bedford County
Joseph Wright Sr.	0	0	1844 Joseph Wright of Hardin County, Kentucky, son of 1815 Joseph Wright of Bedford County and grandson of 1763 Thomas Wright of Bedford County
Wright Wright	0	0	1855 Wright Wright of Franklin County, son of 1815 Joseph Wright of Bedford County and grandson of 1763 Thomas Wright of Bedford County
William Wright	0	4	1830 William Wright of Franklin County, son of 1809 William Wright of Franklin County and probably grandson of 1792 John Wright of Fauquier County
Hyrum Wright	0	3	Hiram Wright, son of 1830 William Wright of Franklin County, grandson of 1809 William Wright of Franklin County, and probably great grandson of 1792 John Wright of Fauquier County
John Wright	0	0	1839 John A. Wright of Franklin County, son of 1830 William Wright of Franklin County, grandson of 1809 William Wright of Franklin County, and probably great grandson of 1792 John Wright of Fauquier County
George Wright	0	0	1843 George Wright of Franklin County, son of 1809 William Wright of Franklin County and probably grandson of 1792 John Wright of Fauquier County

Appendix: Franklin County, Virginia, 1810 Census:

Name of Town, city or County	Names of Heads of families	Free White Males					Free White Females				
		Under ten years of age to 10	Of ten years, and under sixteen to 16	Of sixteen, and under twenty-six including heads of families to 26	Of twenty-six and under forty-five including heads of families to 45	Of forty five and upwards, including heads of families 45&c	Under ten years of age to 10	Of ten years, and under sixteen to 16	Of sixteen, and under twenty six including heads of families to 26	Of twenty-six and under forty five, including heads of families to 45	Of forty-five and upwards, including heads of families 45&c
	Enoch Wright	1	0	1	0	0	1	0	1	0	00
	John Wright Sr.	1	1	2	0	1	0	1	1	0	1
	James Wright	3	1	2	0	1	1	2	2	1	00
	Olaver Wright	2	0	1	0	0	1	1	1	0	0
	John Wright Jr.	3	0	0	1	0	1	0	0	1	00
	Jacob Wright	0	0	1	0	0	0	0	1	0	0

Appendix: Franklin County, Virginia, 1810 Census:

Names of Heads of families [continued from prior page]	All other free persons except Indians, not taxed	Slaves	Identification
Enoch Wright	0	0	1871 Enoch Wright of Tulare County, California, son of _____ Wright, grandson of 1809 William Wright of Franklin County, and probably great grandson of 1792 John Wright of Fauquier County
John Wright Sr.	0	0	1845 John Wright of Franklin County, probably son of 1809 William Wright of Franklin County and grandson of 1792 John Wright of Fauquier County
James Wright	0	0	1823 James Wright of Franklin County, son of 1809 William Wright of Franklin County and probably grandson of 1792 John Wright of Fauquier County
Olaver Wright	0	0	1848 Oliver Wright of Kosciusko County, Indiana, possibly son of 1845 John Wright of Franklin County, grandson of 1809 William Wright of Franklin County, and great grandson of 1792 John Wright of Fauquier County
John Wright Jr.	0	0	1848/50 John Wright of Muhlenberg County, Kentucky, probably son of 1845 John Wright of Franklin County, grandson of 1809 William Wright of Franklin County, and great grandson of 1792 John Wright of Fauquier County
Jacob Wright	0	3	Jacob Wright (Floyd County), son of Joshua Wright

1820 CENSUS

FRANKLIN COUNTY, VIRGINIA

Appendix: Franklin County, Virginia, 1820 Census:

Names of Heads of Families	Free White Males						Free White Females				
	Free white males under ten years to 10	Free white males of ten and under sixteen to 16	Free white males between sixteen and eighteen 16 to 18	Free white males of sixteen and under twenty-six including heads of families 16 to 26	Free white males of twenty-six and under forty-five, including heads of families to 45	Free white males of forty-five and upwards, including heads of families 45, &c.	Free white females under ten years of age to 10	Free white females of ten and under six-teen to 16	Free white females of six-teen and under twenty six, including heads of families to 26	Free white females of twenty-six and under forty-five, including heads of families to 45	Free white females of forty-five, and upwards including heads of families 45, &c.
Thomas Wright Sr.(?)	0	0	1	2	0	1	0	0	0	1	0
George Wright	0	0	0	0	1	0	2	0	1	1	0
James Wright	1	1	0	0	0	1	2	1	1	1	1
Ezekiel Wright	2	1	0	0	1	0	3	0	0	1	0
John Wright	0	0	0	1	1	0	1	0	1	0	0

Appendix: Franklin County, Virginia, 1820 Census:

Names of Heads of Families [continued from prior page]	Foreigners not natur-alized	Number of persons engaged in Agri-culture	Number of persons engaged in Commerce	Number of persons engaged in Manu-facture	Slaves							
					Males				Females			
					Males under fourteen to 14	Males of four-teen and under twenty-six to 26	Males of twenty-six and under forty-five to 45	Males of forty-five and upwards 45, &c.	Females of (under) fourteen to 14	Females of four-teen and under twenty-six to 26	Females of twenty-six and under forty-five to 45	Females of forty-five and upwards 45, &c.
Thomas Wright Sr.(?)	0	0	0	0	0	0	0	0	0	0	0	0
George Wright	0	1	0	0	0	0	0	0	0	0	0	0
James Wright	0	1	0	0	0	0	0	0	0	0	0	0
Ezekiel Wright	0	1	0	0	0	0	0	0	0	0	0	0
John Wright	0	3	0	0	0	0	0	0	1	0	0	0

Appendix: Franklin County, Virginia, 1820 Census:

Names of Heads of Families [continued from prior page]	Free Colored Persons									Identification
	Males				Females					
	Males under four-teen years to 14	Males of four-teen and under twenty-six to 26	Males of twenty-six and under forty-five to 45	Males of forty five and upwards 45, &c	Females under fourteen years to 14	Females of four-teen and under twenty-six to 26	Females of twenty-six and under forty-five to 45	Females of forty-five and upwards 45, &c	All other persons except Indians not taxed	
Thomas Wright Sr.(?)										1849 Thomas Wright of Franklin County, son of 1815 Joseph Wright of Bedford County, grandson of 1763 Thomas Wright of Bedford County
George Wright										George Wright (Stiller), son of 1823 James Wright of Franklin County, grandson of 1809 William Wright of Franklin County and probably great grandson of 1792 John Wright of Fauquier County
James Wright										1823 James Wright of Franklin County, son of 1809 William Wright of Franklin County and probably grandson of 1792 John Wright of Fauquier County
Ezekiel Wright										1874 Ezekiel Wright of Franklin County, son of 1845 John Wright of Franklin County, probably grandson of 1809 William Wright of Franklin County, and great grandson of 1792 John Wright of Fauquier County
John Wright										John Wright, son of 1854 William Wright of Campbell County, grandson of 1814 John Wright of Bedford County, and great grandson of John Wright (Goochland County Carpenter)

Appendix: Franklin County, Virginia, 1820 Census:

Names of Heads of Families	Free White Males						Free White Females				
	Free white males under ten years to 10	Free white males of ten and under sixteen to 16	Free white males between sixteen and eighteen 16 to 18	Free white males of sixteen and under twenty-six including heads of families 16 to 26	Free white males of twenty-six and under forty-five, including heads of families to 45	Free white males of forty-five and upwards, including heads of families 45, &c.	Free white females under ten years of age to 10	Free white females of ten and under six-teen to 16	Free white females of six-teen and under twenty six, including heads of families to 26	Free white females of twenty-six and under forty-five, including heads of families to 45	Free white females of forty-five, and upwards including heads of families 45, &c.
John Wright	4	2	0	0	1	1	2	0	2	1	0
George Wright	2	1	1	1	0	1	2	2	3	0	1
Moses Wright	0	0	0	0	1	0	2	0	1	0	0
Hiram Wright	3	0	0	0	1	0	2	1	0	1	0

Appendix: Franklin County, Virginia, 1820 Census:

Names of Heads of Families [continued from prior page]	Foreigners not natur- alized	Number of persons engaged in Agri- culture	Number of persons engaged in Commerce	Number of persons engaged in Manu- facture	Slaves							
					Males				Females			
					Males under fourteen to 14	Males of four- teen and under twenty- six to 26	Males of twenty- six and under forty- five to 45	Males of forty- five and upwards 45, &c.	Females of (under) fourteen to 14	Females of four- teen and under twenty- six to 26	Females of twenty- six and under forty- five to 45	Females of forty- five and upwards 45, &c.
John Wright	0	3	0	0	0	0	0	0	1	0	1	0
George Wright	0	4	0	0	0	0	0	0	0	0	0	0
Moses Wright	0	1	0	0	0	0	0	0	0	0	0	0
Hiram Wright	0	6	0	0	0	0	2	0	0	1	0	1

Appendix: Franklin County, Virginia, 1820 Census:

	Free Colored Persons									
	Males				Females					
Names of Heads of Families [continued from prior page]	Males under four-teen years to 14	Males of four-teen and under twenty-six to 26	Males of twenty-six and under forty-five to 45	Males of forty five and upwards 45, &c	Females under fourteen years to 14	Females of four-teen and under twenty-six to 26	Females of twenty-six and under forty-five to 45	Females of forty-five and upwards 45, &c	All other persons except Indians not taxed	Identification
John Wright										1839 John A. Wright of Franklin County, son of 1830 William Wright of Franklin County, grandson of 1809 William Wright of Franklin County, and probably great grandson of 1792 John Wright of Fauquier County
George Wright										1843 George Wright of Franklin County, son of 1809 William Wright of Franklin County and probably grandson of 1792 John Wright of Fauquier County
Moses Wright										Moses Wright, son of 1843 George Wright of Franklin County, grandson of 1809 William Wright of Franklin County, and probably great grandson of 1792 John Wright of Fauquier County
Hiram Wright										Hiram Wright, son of 1830 William Wright of Franklin County, grandson of 1809 William Wright of Franklin County, and probably great grandson of 1792 John Wright of Fauquier County

Appendix: Franklin County, Virginia, 1820 Census:

Names of Heads of Families	Free White Males						Free White Females				
	Free white males under ten years to 10	Free white males of ten and under sixteen to 16	Free white males between sixteen and eighteen 16 to 18	Free white males of sixteen and under twenty-six including heads of families 16 to 26	Free white males of twenty-six and under forty-five, including heads of families to 45	Free white males of forty-five and upwards, including heads of families 45, &c.	Free white females under ten years of age to 10	Free white females of ten and under six-teen to 16	Free white females of six-teen and under twenty six, including heads of families to 26	Free white females of twenty-six and under forty-five, including heads of families to 45	Free white females of forty-five, and upwards including heads of families 45, &c.
William Wright	1	0	0	1	0	1	0	1	1	0	1
John Wright	0	2	0	1	0	1	0	1	1	0	1
Ambrose Wright	1	0	0	0	1	0	1	0	1	0	0
Grief Wright	3	0	0	0	1	0	1	0	1	0	0
Right Wright	1	0	0	0	1	0	1	1	0	1	0
William Wright	0	0	0	1	0	1	0	0	2	2	1

Appendix: Franklin County, Virginia, 1820 Census:

Names of Heads of Families [continued from prior page]	Foreigners not naturalized	Number of persons engaged in Agriculture	Number of persons engaged in Commerce	Number of persons engaged in Manufacture	Slaves							
					Males				Females			
					Males under fourteen to 14	Males of fourteen and under twenty-six to 26	Males of twenty-six and under forty-five to 45	Males of forty-five and upwards 45, &c.	Females of (under) fourteen to 14	Females of fourteen and under twenty-six to 26	Females of twenty-six and under forty-five to 45	Females of forty-five and upwards 45, &c.
William Wright	0	5	0	0	0	1	0	0	2	1	0	1
John Wright	0	3	0	0	0	0	0	0	0	0	0	0
Ambrose Wright	0	1	0	0	0	0	0	0	0	0	0	0
Grief Wright	0	1	0	0	0	0	0	0	0	0	0	0
Right Wright	0	4	0	0	0	0	0	0	0	1	2	1
William Wright	0	10	0	0	3	1	1	0	0	4	2	0

Appendix: Franklin County, Virginia, 1820 Census:

	Free Colored Persons									
	Males				Females					
Names of Heads of Families [continued from prior page]	Males under four- teen years to 14	Males of four- teen and under twenty- six to 26	Males of twenty- six and under forty- five to 45	Males of forty five and upwards 45, &c	Females under fourteen years to 14	Females of four- teen and under twenty- six to 26	Females of twenty- six and under forty- five to 45	Females of forty- five and upwards 45, &c	All other persons except Indians not taxed	Identification
William Wright										1854 William Wright of Campbell County, son of 1814 John Wright of Bedford County and grandson of John Wright (Goochland County Carpenter)
John Wright										1845 John Wright of Franklin County, probably son of 1809 William Wright of Franklin County and grandson of 1792 John Wright of Fauquier County
Ambrose Wright										
Grief Wright										Grief Wright (Bedford County)
Right Wright										1855 Wright Wright of Franklin County, son of 1815 Joseph Wright of Bedford County and grandson of 1763 Thomas Wright of Bedford County
William Wright										1830 William Wright of Franklin County, son of 1809 William Wright of Franklin County, and probably grandson of 1792 John Wright of Fauquier County

Appendix: Franklin County, Virginia, 1820 Census:

Names of Heads of Families	Free White Males						Free White Females				
	Free white males under ten years to 10	Free white males of ten and under sixteen to 16	Free white males between sixteen and eighteen 16 to 18	Free white males of sixteen and under twenty-six including heads of families 16 to 26	Free white males of twenty-six and under forty-five, including heads of families to 45	Free white males of forty-five and upwards, including heads of families 45, &c.	Free white females under ten years of age to 10	Free white females of ten and under sixteen to 16	Free white females of six-teen and under twenty six, including heads of families to 26	Free white females of twenty-six and under forty-five, including heads of families to 45	Free white females of forty-five, and upwards including heads of families 45, &c.
Thomas Wright	1	0	0	1	0	0	0	0	1	0	0
James Wright	0	0	0	0	1	0	0	0	1	0	0
David Wright	4	0	0	0	1	0	1	0	1	0	0
Joseph Wright	0	0	0	0	0	1	0	0	0	0	1

Appendix: Franklin County, Virginia, 1820 Census:

| | | | | | Slaves | | | | | | | |
| | | | | | Males | | | | Females | | | |
Names of Heads of Families [continued from prior page]	Foreigners not naturalized	Number of persons engaged in Agriculture	Number of persons engaged in Commerce	Number of persons engaged in Manufacture	Males under fourteen to 14	Males of fourteen and under twenty-six to 26	Males of twenty-six and under forty-five to 45	Males of forty-five and upwards 45, &c.	Females of (under) fourteen to 14	Females of fourteen and under twenty-six to 26	Females of twenty-six and under forty-five to 45	Females of forty-five and upwards 45, &c.
Thomas Wright	0	1	0	0	1	0	0	0	0	0	0	0
James Wright	0	3	0	0	0	0	1	0	1	1	0	0
David Wright	0	1	0	0	0	0	0	0	0	0	0	0
Joseph Wright	0	1	0	0	0	0	0	0	0	0	0	0

Appendix: Franklin County, Virginia, 1820 Census:

	Free Colored Persons									
	Males				Females					
Names of Heads of Families [continued from prior page]	Males under fourteen years to 14	Males of fourteen and under twenty-six to 26	Males of twenty-six and under forty-five to 45	Males of forty five and upwards 45, &c	Females under fourteen years to 14	Females of fourteen and under twenty-six to 26	Females of twenty-six and under forty-five to 45	Females of forty-five and upwards 45, &c	All other persons except Indians not taxed	Identification
Thomas Wright										Thomas Anthony Wright of Arkansas, son of 1849 Thomas Wright of Franklin County, grandson of 1815 Joseph Wright of Bedford County, and great grandson of 1763 Thomas Wright of Bedford County
James Wright										1857 James Wright of Delaware County, Indiana, son of 1830 William Wright of Franklin County. grandson of 1809 William Wright of Franklin County, and probably great grandson of 1792 John Wright of Fauquier County
David Wright										David Wright, son of 1844 Joseph Wright of Hardin County, Kentucky, grandson of 1815 Joseph Wright of Bedford County, and great grandson of 1763 Thomas Wright of Bedford County
Joseph Wright										1844 Joseph Wright of Hardin County, Kentucky, son of 1815 Joseph Wright of Bedford County and grandson of 1763 Thomas Wright of Bedford County

Appendix: Franklin County, Virginia, 1820 Census:

Names of Heads of Families	Free White Males						Free White Females				
	Free white males under ten years to 10	Free white males of ten and under sixteen to 16	Free white males between sixteen and eighteen 16 to 18	Free white males of sixteen and under twenty-six including heads of families 16 to 26	Free white males of twenty-six and under forty-five, including heads of families to 45	Free white males of forty-five and upwards, including heads of families 45, &c.	Free white females under ten years of age to 10	Free white females of ten and under sixteen to 16	Free white females of sixteen and under twenty six, including heads of families to 26	Free white females of twenty-six and under forty-five, including heads of families to 45	Free white females of forty-five, and upwards including heads of families 45, &c.
Martin Wright	1	0	0	1	0	0	3	0	1	0	0
George Wright	2	0	1	1	1	0	0	0	0	1	0

Appendix: Franklin County, Virginia, 1820 Census:

Names of Heads of Families [continued from prior page]	Foreigners not natur-alized	Number of persons engaged in Agri-culture	Number of persons engaged in Commerce	Number of persons engaged in Manu-facture	Slaves							
					Males				Females			
					Males under fourteen to 14	Males of four-teen and under twenty-six to 26	Males of twenty-six and under forty-five to 45	Males of forty-five and upwards 45, &c.	Females of (under) fourteen to 14	Females of four-teen and under twenty-six to 26	Females of twenty-six and under forty-five to 45	Females of forty-five and upwards 45, &c.
Martin Wright	0	1	0	0	0	0	0	0	0	0	0	0
George Wright	0	1	0	0	0	0	0	0	0	0	0	0

Appendix: Franklin County, Virginia, 1820 Census:

Names of Heads of Families [continued from prior page]	Free Colored Persons									Identification
	Males				Females					
	Males under four-teen years to 14	Males of four-teen and under twenty-six to 26	Males of twenty-six and under forty-five to 45	Males of forty five and upwards 45, &c	Females under fourteen years to 14	Females of four-teen and under twenty-six to 26	Females of twenty-six and under forty-five to 45	Females of forty-five and upwards 45, &c	All other persons except Indians not taxed	
Martin Wright										1856 Martin G. Wright of Hardin County Kentucky, son of 1844 Joseph Wright of Hardin County, Kentucky, grandson of 1815 Joseph Wright of Bedford County, and great grandson of 1763 Thomas Wright of Bedford County
George Wright										George Finney Wright, son of 1830 William Wright of Franklin County, grandson of 1809 William Wright of Franklin County, and probably great grandson of 1792 John Wright of Fauquier County

1830 CENSUS

FRANKLIN COUNTY, VIRGINIA

Appendix: Franklin County, Virginia, 1830 Census

| | Free White Persons (including heads of families) | | | | | | | | | | | | |
| | Males | | | | | | | | | | | | |
Names Heads of Families	Under five years of age under 5	Of five and under ten 5 to 10	Of ten and under fifteen 10 to 15	Of fifteen and under twenty 15 to 20	Of twenty and under thirty 20 to 30	Of thirty and under forty 30 to 40	Of forty and under fifty 40 to 50	Of fifty and under sixty 50 to 60	Of sixty and under seventy 60 to 70	Of seventy and under eighty 70 to 80	Of eighty and under ninety 80 to 90	Of ninety and under one hundred 90 to 100	Of one hundred and upwards 100, &c.
John Wright	3	1	1	2	2	0	0	1	0	0	0	0	0
Ambrose Wright	1	2	0	0	0	1	0	0	0	0	0	0	0
Washington Wright	0	0	0	0	1	1	0	0	0	0	0	0	0
Wright Wright	1	1	0	0	1	0	1	0	0	0	0	0	0
Thomas Wright Sr.	0	1	0	0	0	0	0	0	1	0	0	0	0
George Wright	2	1	2	0	1	0	1	1	0	0	0	0	0
Pendleton Wright	1	0	0	0	0	1	0	0	0	0	0	0	0
George Finay Wright	0	0	1	1	0	1	0	0	0	0	0	0	0
Nancy Wright	0	0	0	0	1	0	0	0	0	0	0	0	0
William Wright Jr.	1	0	0	0	0	1	0	0	0	0	0	0	0

Appendix: Franklin County, Virginia, 1830 Census

Names Heads of Families [Continued from prior page]	Free White Persons (including heads of families) [Continued] Females												
	Under five years of age under 5	Of five and under ten 5 to 10	Of ten and under fifteen 10 to 15	Of fifteen and under twenty 15 to 20	Of twenty and under thirty 20 to 30	Of thirty and under forty 30 to 40	Of forty and under fifty 40 to 50	Of fifty and under sixty 50 to 60	Of sixty and under seventy 60 to 70	Of seventy and under eighty 70 to 80	Of eighty and under ninety 80 to 90	Of ninety and under one hundred 90 to 100	Of one hundred and upwards 100, &c.
John Wright	1	0	1	0	0	0	1	0	0	0	0	0	0
Ambrose Wright	1	0	1	0	1	0	0	0	0	0	0	0	0
Washington Wright	1	0	0	0	1	0	0	0	0	0	0	0	0
Wright Wright	0	0	1	1	0	0	1	0	1	0	0	0	0
Thomas Wright Sr.	0	0	0	0	0	0	0	1	0	0	0	0	0
George Wright	0	1	0	2	1	0	0	1	0	0	0	0	0
Pendleton Wright	2	0	0	0	1	0	0	0	0	0	0	0	0
George Finay Wright	0	0	0	0	0	1	0	0	0	0	0	0	0
Nancy Wright	0	0	0	0	0	0	2	0	0	1	0	0	0
William Wright Jr.	1	0	0	0	1	0	0	0	0	0	0	0	0

Appendix: Franklin County, Virginia, 1830 Census

Names Heads of Families [Continued from prior page]	Slaves											
	Males						Females					
	Under ten years of age under 10	Of ten and under twenty-four 10 to 24	Of twenty-four and under thirty-six 24 to 36	Of thirty-six and under fifty-five 36 to 55	Of fifty-five and under one hundred 55 to 100	Of one hundred and upwards 100, &c	Under ten years of age under 10	Of ten and under twenty-four 10 to 24	Of twenty-four and under thirty-six 24 to 36	Of thirty-six and under fifty-five 36 to 55	Of fifty-five and under one hundred 55 to 100	Of one hundred and upwards 100, &c
John Wright	1	0	1	0	0	0	1	1	0	1	0	0
Ambrose Wright	0	0	0	0	0	0	0	0	0	0	0	0
Washington Wright	0	0	0	0	0	0	0	0	0	0	0	0
Wright Wright	0	0	0	1	0	0	0	0	2	0	1	0
Thomas Wright Sr.	1	2	0	0	0	0	0	2	0	1	0	0
George Wright	0	1	0	0	0	0	0	0	0	1	0	0
Pendleton Wright	1	0	0	0	0	0	0	0	1	0	0	0
George Finay Wright	1	0	0	0	0	0	0	1	0	1	0	0
Nancy Wright	3	1	1	0	0	0	3	3	3	1	0	0
William Wright Jr.	1	0	0	0	0	0	0	3	0	0	0	0

Appendix: Franklin County, Virginia, 1830 Census

	Free Colored Persons											
	Males						Females					
Names Heads of Families [Continued from prior page]	Under ten years of age under 10	Of ten and under twenty-four 10 to 24	Of twenty-four and under thirty-six 24 to 36	Of thirty-six and under fifty-five 36 to 55	Of fifty-five and under one hundred 55 to 100	Of one hundred and upwards 100, &c	Under ten years of age under 10	Of ten and under twenty-four 10 to 24	Of twenty-four and under thirty-six 24 to 36	Of thirty-six and under fifty-five 36 to 55	Of fifty-five and under one hundred 55 to 100	Of one hundred and upwards 100, &c
John Wright	0	0	0	0	0	0	0	0	0	0	0	0
Ambrose Wright	0	0	0	0	0	0	0	0	0	0	0	0
Washington Wright	0	0	0	0	0	0	0	0	0	0	0	0
Wright Wright	0	0	0	0	0	0	0	0	0	0	0	0
Thomas Wright Sr.	0	0	0	0	0	0	0	0	0	0	0	0
George Wright	0	0	0	0	0	0	0	0	0	0	0	0
Pendleton Wright	0	0	0	0	0	0	0	0	0	0	0	0
George Finay Wright	0	0	0	0	1	0	0	0	0	0	0	0
Nancy Wright	0	0	0	0	0	0	0	0	0	0	0	0
William Wright Jr.	0	0	0	0	0	0	0	0	0	0	0	0

Appendix: Franklin County, Virginia, 1830 Census

Names Heads of Families [Continued from prior page]	Total	White Persons included in the foregoing					Slaves and Colored Persons, included in the foregoing			
		Who are Deaf and Dumb, under fourteen years of age under 14	Who are Deaf and Dumb, of the age of fourteen and under twenty-five 14 to 25	Who are Deaf and Dumb, of twenty-five and upwards 25, &c.	Who are blind	Aliens - Foreigners and naturalized	Who are Deaf and Dumb, under fourteen years of age under 14	Who are Deaf and Dumb, of the age of fourteen and under twenty-five 14-25	Who are Deaf and Dumb of twenty-five and upwards 25, &c.	Who are blind
John Wright	18									
Ambrose Wright	7									
Washington Wright	4									
Wright Wright	12									
Thomas Wright Sr.	10									
George Wright	15									
Pendleton Wright	5									
George Finay Wright	8									
Nancy Wright	19									
William Wright Jr.	8									

Appendix: Franklin County, Virginia, 1830 Census

Names
Heads of Families
[Continued from
prior page]   Identification

John Wright   1839 John A. Wright of Franklin County, son of 1830 William Wright of Franklin County, grandson of 1809 William Wright of Franklin County, and probably great grandson of 1792 John Wright of Fauquier County

Ambrose Wright

Washington Wright   George Washington Wright, son of 1843 George Wright of Franklin County, grandson of 1809 William Wright of Franklin County, and probably great grandson of 1792 John Wright of Fauquier County

Wright Wright   1855 Wright Wright of Franklin County, son of 1815 Joseph Wright of Bedford County and grandson of 1763 Thomas Wright of Bedford County

Thomas Wright Sr.   1849 Thomas Wright of Franklin County, son of 1815 Joseph Wright of Bedford County and grandson of 1763 Thomas Wright of Bedford County

George Wright   1843 George Wright of Franklin County, son of 1809 William Wright of Franklin County and probably grandson of 1792 John Wright of Fauquier County

Pendleton Wright   1864 Pendleton Wright of Hamilton County, Indiana, son of 1843 George Wright of Franklin County, grandson of 1809 William Wright of Franklin County, and probably great grandson of 1792 John Wright of Fauquier County

George Finay Wright   George Finney Wright, son of 1830 William Wright of Franklin County, grandson of 1809 William Wright of Franklin County, and probably great grandson of 1792 John Wright of Fauquier County

Nancy Wright   Nancy Wright, daughter of 1830 William Wright of Franklin County, granddaughter of 1809 William Wright of Franklin County, and probably great granddaughter of 1792 John Wright of Fauquier County

William Wright Jr.   1845 William Wright of Franklin County, son of 1830 William Wright of Franklin County, grandson of 1804 William Wright of Franklin County, and probably great grandson of 1792 John Wright of Fauquier County

Appendix: Franklin County, Virginia, 1830 Census

Names Heads of Families	Free White Persons (including heads of families)													
	Males													
	Under five years of age under 5	Of five and under ten 5 to 10	Of ten and under fifteen 10 to 15	Of fifteen and under twenty 15 to 20	Of twenty and under thirty 20 to 30	Of thirty and under forty 30 to 40	Of forty and under fifty 40 to 50	Of fifty and under sixty 50 to 60	Of sixty and under seventy 60 to 70	Of seventy and under eighty 70 to 80	Of eighty and under ninety 80 to 90	Of ninety and under one hundred 90 to 100	Of one hundred and upwards 100, &c.
James G. Wright	0	1	0	1	2	1	0	0	0	0	0	0	0
John Wright Sr.	0	0	0	0	0	0	0	0	0	0	1	0	0
Ansolem Wright	2	0	0	0	1	0	0	0	0	0	0	0	0
Joseph Wright Jr.	1	0	0	0	0	1	0	0	0	0	0	0	0
James Wright	2	0	0	0	0	0	1	0	0	0	0	0	0
Ezekiel Wright	0	0	1	1	0	0	1	0	0	0	0	0	0
William Wright B.W.	0	0	0	1	0	0	0	0	1	0	0	0	0

Names Heads of Families [Continued from prior page]	Free White Persons (including heads of families) [Continued]												
	Females												
	Under five years of age under 5	Of five and under ten 5 to 10	Of ten and under fifteen 10 to 15	Of fifteen and under twenty 15 to 20	Of twenty and under thirty 20 to 30	Of thirty and under forty 30 to 40	Of forty and under fifty 40 to 50	Of fifty and under sixty 50 to 60	Of sixty and under seventy 60 to 70	Of seventy and under eighty 70 to 80	Of eighty and under ninety 80 to 90	Of ninety and under one hundred 90 to 100	Of one hundred and upwards 100, &c.
James G. Wright	0	0	0	0	2	1	0	0	1	0	0	0	0
John Wright Sr.	0	0	0	0	0	0	0	0	0	1	0	0	0
Ansolem Wright	0	0	0	0	1	0	0	0	0	0	0	0	0
Joseph Wright Jr.	1	0	0	0	0	1	0	0	0	0	0	0	0
James Wright	1	2	0	1	0	1	0	0	0	0	0	0	0
Ezekiel Wright	2	2	1	1	0	1	0	0	0	0	0	0	0
William Wright B.W.	0	0	0	0	1	0	0	0	0	0	0	0	0

Names Heads of Families [Continued from prior page]	Slaves											
	Males						Females					
	Under ten years of age under 10	Of ten and under twenty-four 10 to 24	Of twenty-four and under thirty-six 24 to 36	Of thirty-six and under fifty-five 36 to 55	Of fifty-five and under one hundred 55 to 100	Of one hundred and upwards 100, &c	Under ten years of age under 10	Of ten and under twenty-four 10 to 24	Of twenty-four and under thirty-six 24 to 36	Of thirty-six and under fifty-five 36 to 55	Of fifty-five and under one hundred 55 to 100	Of one hundred and upwards 100, &c
James G. Wright	0	0	0	0	0	0	0	0	0	0	0	0
John Wright Sr.	0	1	0	0	0	0	0	0	0	0	0	0
Ansolem Wright	0	0	0	0	0	0	0	0	0	0	0	0
Joseph Wright Jr.	0	0	0	0	1	0	0	0	0	0	0	0
James Wright	2	0	1	0	0	0	0	1	0	0	0	0
Ezekiel Wright	0	0	0	0	0	0	0	0	0	0	0	0
William Wright B.W.	2	0	1	0	0	0	4	1	1	0	1	0

Appendix: Franklin County, Virginia, 1830 Census

	Free Colored Persons											
	Males						Females					
Names Heads of Families [Continued from prior page]	Under ten years of age under 10	Of ten and under twenty-four 10 to 24	Of twenty-four and under thirty-six 24 to 36	Of thirty-six and under fifty-five 36 to 55	Of fifty-five and under one hundred 55 to 100	Of one hundred and upwards 100, &c	Under ten years of age under 10	Of ten and under twenty-four 10 to 24	Of twenty-four and under thirty-six 24 to 36	Of thirty-six and under fifty-five 36 to 55	Of fifty-five and under one hundred 55 to 100	Of one hundred and upwards 100, &c
James G. Wright	0	0	0	0	0	0	0	0	0	0	0	0
John Wright Sr.												
Ansolem Wright												
Joseph Wright Jr.												
James Wright												
Ezekiel Wright												
William Wright B.W.												

Appendix: Franklin County, Virginia, 1830 Census

Names Heads of Families [Continued from prior page]	Total	White Persons included in the foregoing					Slaves and Colored Persons, included in the foregoing			
		Who are Deaf and Dumb, under fourteen years of age under 14	Who are Deaf and Dumb, of the age of fourteen and under twenty-five 14 to 25	Who are Deaf and Dumb, of twenty-five and upwards 25, &c.	Who are blind	Aliens - Foreigners and naturalized	Who are Deaf and Dumb, under fourteen years of age under 14	Who are Deaf and Dumb, of the age of fourteen and under twenty-five 14-25	Who are Deaf and Dumb of twenty-five and upwards 25, &c.	Who are blind
James G. Wright	9									
John Wright Sr.	3									
Ansolem Wright	4									
Joseph Wright Jr.	5									
James Wright	12									
Ezekiel Wright	10									
William Wright B.W.	13									

Appendix: Franklin County, Virginia, 1830 Census

Names
Heads of Families
[Continued from
prior page]   Identification

James G. Wright   James Grant Wright, son of 1823 James Wright of Franklin County, grandson of 1809 William Wright of Franklin County, and probably great grandson of 1792 John Wright of Fauquier County

John Wright Sr.   1845 John Wright of Franklin County, probably son of 1809 William Wright of Franklin County and grandson of 1792 John Wright of Fauquier County

Ansolem Wright   1883 Anslem Wright of Franklin County, son of William Wright

Joseph Wright Jr.   Joseph Wright, son of 1845 John Wright of Franklin County, probably grandson of 1809 William Wright of Franklin County, and great grandson of 1792 John Wright of Fauquier County

James Wright   1857 James Wright of Delaware County, Indiana, son of 1830 William Wright of Franklin County, grandson of 1809 William Wright of Franklin County, and probably great grandson of 1792 John Wright of Fauquier County

Ezekiel Wright   1874 Ezekiel Wright of Franklin County, son of 1845 John Wright of Franklin County, probably grandson of 1809 William Wright of Franklin County, and great grandson of 1792 John Wright of Fauquier County

William Wright B.W.   1854 William Wright of Campbell County, son of 1814 John Wright of Bedford County and grandson of John Wright (Goochland County Carpenter)

0304(102201)

1840 CENSUS

FRANKLIN COUNTY, VIRGINIA

Names of Heads of Families	Under 5	5 & under 10	10 & under 15	15 & under 20	20 & under 30	30 & under 40	40 & under 50	50 & under 60	60 & under 70	70 & under 80	80 & under 90	90 & under 100	100 and upwards
				Free White Persons (including heads of families) Males									
Wm Wright Jr	2	0	0	0	1	0	0	0	0	0	0	0	0
Wm Wright	0	0	0	0	1	0	0	0	0	1	0	0	0
Joseph Wright	0	0	1	0	0	0	1	0	0	0	0	0	0
George Wright	0	0	2	0	1	0	0	0	0	1	0	0	0
Ansolem Wright	1	0	2	0	0	0	1	0	0	0	0	0	0
Ezekiel Wright	0	0	0	0	1	0	0	1	0	0	0	0	0
Margaret Wright	0	0	0	0	0	0	0	0	0	0	0	0	0
George L Wright	0	0	0	1	1	1	1	0	0	0	0	0	0
James G Wright	1	1	0	0	0	0	1	0	0	0	0	0	0

Appendix: Franklin County, Virginia, 1840 Census

Names of Heads of Families [Continued from prior page]	Under 5	5 & under 10	10 & under 15	15 & under 20	20 & under 30	30 & under 40	40 & under 50	50 & under 60	60 & under 70	70 & under 80	80 & under 90	90 & under 100	100 and upwards
Wm Wright Jr	0	0	0	0	0	1	0	0	0	0	0	0	0
Wm Wright	1	0	0	1	0	0	0	0	0	0	0	0	0
Joseph Wright	0	0	0	1	0	0	1	0	0	0	1	0	0
George Wright	0	0	1	2	0	0	0	0	1	0	0	0	0
Ansolem Wright	3	2	0	0	0	1	0	0	0	0	0	0	0
Ezekiel Wright	0	0	1	2	0	0	0	1	0	0	0	0	0
Margaret Wright	0	0	0	0	0	0	1	1	0	0	0	0	0
George L Wright	0	1	2	1	1	0	1	0	0	0	0	0	0
James G Wright	1	1	0	0	0	0	0	0	0	0	0	0	0

The header above the table reads: Free White Persons (including heads of families) [Continued] — Females

Appendix: Franklin County, Virginia, 1840 Census

Names of Heads of Families [Continued from prior page]	Free Colored Persons											
	Males						Females					
	Under 10	10 & under 24	24 & under 36	36 & under 55	55 & under 100	100 & and upwards	5 & under 10	10 & under 24	24 & under 36	36 & under 55	55 & under 100	100 and upwards
Wm Wright Jr												
Wm Wright												
Joseph Wright												
George Wright												
Ansolem Wright												
Ezekiel Wright												
Margaret Wright												
George L Wright												
James G Wright												

Appendix: Franklin County, Virginia, 1840 Census

| Names of Heads of Families [Continued from prior page] | Slaves | | | | | | | | | | | | |
| | Males | | | | | | Females | | | | | | |
	Under 10	10 & under 24	24 & under 36	36 & under 55	55 & under 100	100 and upwards	Under 10	10 & under 24	24 & under 36	36 & under 55	55 & under 100	100 and upwards	Total
Wm Wright Jr	0	0	0	0	0	0	0	0	0	0	0	0	4
Wm Wright	3	2	1	0	0	0	3	2	1	0	1	0	17
Joseph Wright	0	0	0	0	0	0	0	0	0	0	0	0	5
George Wright	0	0	0	0	0	0	0	0	0	0	0	0	4
Ansolem Wright	0	0	0	0	0	0	0	0	0	0	0	0	10
Ezekiel Wright	0	0	0	0	0	0	0	0	0	0	0	0	6
Margaret Wright	0	0	0	0	0	0	0	0	0	0	0	0	2
George L Wright	0	0	0	0	0	0	0	0	0	0	0	0	9
James G Wright	0	0	0	0	0	0	0	0	0	0	0	0	6

Appendix: Franklin County, Virginia, 1840 Census

Names of Heads of Families [Continued from prior page]	Mining	Agri-culture	Commerce	Manu-facture and trades	Navi-gation of the ocean	Navi-gation of canals lakes and rivers	Learned profes-sions and engineers	Pensioners for Revolutionary or Military Ser-vices Included in the foregoing Names	Ages	Deaf and Dumb Under 14	14 & under 25	25 and upwards	Blind	Insane and idiots at public charge	Insane and idiots at private charge
Wm Wright Jr		1													
Wm Wright		3		5											
Joseph Wright		2													
George Wright		1													
Ansolem Wright		3													
Ezekiel Wright		2													
Margaret Wright															
George L Wright		3													
James G Wright				2											

Appendix: Franklin County, Virginia, 1840 Census

| Names of Heads of Families [Continued from prior page] | Deaf and Dumb, Blind and Insane Colored Persons Included in the Foregoing | | | | Schools, &c. | | | | | | |
| | Deaf, Dumb, and Blind | | Insane and Idiots | | | | | | | | |
	Deaf & Dumb	Blind	Insane and idiots at private charge	Insane and idiots at public charge	Universities or College	Number of Students	Academies & Grammar Schools	No. of Scholars	Primary and Common Schools	No. of Scholars	No. of Scholars at public charge
Wm Wright Jr											
Wm Wright											
Joseph Wright											
George Wright											
Ansolem Wright											1
Ezekiel Wright											
Margaret Wright											2
George L Wright											2
James G Wright											

Appendix: Franklin County, Virginia, 1840 Census

Names of Heads of Families [Continued from prior page]	No. of white persons over 90 years of age in each family who cannot read or write	Identification
Wm Wright Jr		
Wm Wright		1854 William Wright of Franklin County, son of 1814 John Wright of Bedford County and grandson of John Wright (Goochland County Carpenter)
Joseph Wright		Joseph Wright, son of 1845 John Wright of Franklin County, probably grandson of 1809 William Wright of Franklin County, and great grandson of 1792 John Wright of Fauquier County
George Wright		1843 George Wright of Franklin County, son of 1809 William Wright of Franklin County and probably grandson of 1792 John Wright of Fauquier County
Ansolem Wright		1883 Anslem Wright of Franklin County, son of William Wright
Ezekiel Wright		1874 Ezekiel Wright of Franklin County, son of 1845 John Wright of Franklin County, probably grandson of 1809 William Wright of Franklin County, and great grandson of 1792 John Wright of Fauquier County
Margaret Wright		Margaret "Peggy" (Young) Wright, widow of 1823 James Wright of Franklin County, a son of 1809 William Wright of Franklin County and probably grandson of 1792 John Wright of Fauquier County
George L Wright		George Wright (Stiller), son of 1823 James Wright of Franklin County, grandson of 1809 William Wright of Franklin County, and probably great grandson of 1792 John Wright of Fauquier County
James G Wright		James Grant Wright, son of 1823 James Wright of Franklin County, grandson of 1809 William Wright of Franklin County, and probably great grandson of 1792 John Wright of Fauquier County

Names of Heads of Families	Free White Persons (including heads of families) Males												
	Under 5	5 & under 10	10 & under 15	15 & under 20	20 & under 30	30 & under 40	40 & under 50	50 & under 60	60 & under 70	70 & under 80	80 & under 90	90 & under 100	100 and upwards
John B Wright	1	2	0	0	1	0	0	0	0	0	0	0	0
George F Wright	0	0	0	0	2	0	0	1	0	0	0	0	0
Rite Wright	0	0	1	1	1	0	0	0	1	0	0	0	0
George W Wright	1	1	0	0	0	1	0	0	0	0	0	0	0
George A Wright	0	0	0	0	1	0	0	0	0	0	0	0	0
Joseph Wright	0	0	0	0	0	1	0	0	0	0	0	0	0
Elizabeth Wright	0	0	1	2	1	1	0	0	0	0	0	0	0
Wm Wright	0	0	0	1	0	0	0	0	0	0	0	0	0
John Wright	0	0	1	1	0	0	0	0	0	0	0	1	0

Appendix: Franklin County, Virginia, 1840 Census

| | | | | | | Free White Persons (including heads of families) [Continued] | | | | | | | |
| | | | | | | Females | | | | | | | |
Names of Heads of Families [Continued from prior page]	Under 5	5 & under 10	10 & under 15	15 & under 20	20 & under 30	30 & under 40	40 & under 50	50 & under 60	60 & under 70	70 & under 80	80 & under 90	90 & under 100	100 and upwards
John B Wright	1	0	1	1	0	0	0	0	0	0	0	0	0
George F Wright	0	0	0	0	0	0	0	0	0	0	0	0	0
Rite Wright	0	0	1	0	1	0	0	1	0	0	0	0	0
George W Wright	2	1	1	0	0	1	0	0	0	0	0	0	0
George A Wright	1	0	0	1	0	0	0	0	0	0	0	0	0
Joseph Wright	0	0	0	0	1	0	0	0	0	0	0	0	0
Elizabeth Wright	0	0	0	0	0	0	0	1	0	0	0	0	0
Wm Wright	0	0	0	0	1	0	0	0	0	0	0	0	0
John Wright	0	0	0	1	0	0	0	0	0	0	0	1	0

Names of Heads of Families [Continued from prior page]	Free Colored Persons											
	Males						Females					
	Under 10	10 & under 24	24 & under 36	36 & under 55	55 & under 100	100 & and upwards	5 & under 10	10 & under 24	24 & under 36	36 & under 55	55 & under 100	100 and upwards
John B Wright												
George F Wright												
Rite Wright												
George W Wright												
George A Wright												
Joseph Wright												
Elizabeth Wright												
Wm Wright												
John Wright												

Appendix: Franklin County, Virginia, 1840 Census

| | Slaves | | | | | | | | | | | |
| | Males | | | | | | Females | | | | | |
Names of Heads of Families [Continued from prior page]	Under 10	10 & under 24	24 & under 36	36 & under 55	55 & under 100	100 and upwards	Under 10	10 & under 24	24 & under 36	36 & under 55	55 & under 100	100 and upwards	Total
John B Wright	0	0	0	0	0	0	0	0	0	0	0	0	7
George F Wright	0	3	4	0	0	0	0	2	4	2	0	0	18
Rite Wright	0	0	0	0	0	0	0	0	1	1	1	0	10
George W Wright	0	0	0	0	0	0	0	0	0	0	0	0	8
George A Wright	0	0	0	0	0	0	0	0	0	0	0	0	3
Joseph Wright	0	0	0	0	0	0	0	1	0	0	0	0	3
Elizabeth Wright	1	1	0	1	0	0	0	2	0	1	0	0	12
Wm Wright	0	0	0	0	0	0	0	0	0	0	0	0	2
John Wright	0	0	0	0	0	0	0	0	0	0	0	0	5

Appendix: Franklin County, Virginia, 1840 Census

Names of Heads of Families [Continued from prior page]	Number of Persons in each Family Employed in							Pensioners for Revolutionary or Military Services Included in the foregoing		Deaf and Dumb, Blind and Insane White Persons Included in the Foregoing					
										Deaf and Dumb				Insane and Idiots	
	Mining	Agri- culture	Commerce	Manu- facture and trades	Navi- gation of the ocean	Navi- gation of canals lakes and rivers	Learned profes- sions and engineers	Names	Ages	Under 14	14 & under 25	25 and upwards	Blind	Insane and idiots at public charge	Insane and idiots at private charge
John B Wright				1											
George F Wright		8													
Rite Wright		5													
George W Wright		2													
George A Wright		1													
Joseph Wright		2													
Elizabeth Wright		10													
Wm Wright		1													
John Wright		3						John Wright	94						

Appendix: Franklin County, Virginia, 1840 Census

Names of Heads of Families [Continued from prior page]	Deaf and Dumb, Blind and Insane Colored Persons Included in the Foregoing					Schools, &c.						
	Deaf, Dumb, and Blind		Insane and Idiots									
	Deaf & Dumb	Blind	Insane and idiots at private charge	Insane and idiots at public charge	Univer-sities or College	Number of Students	Acade-mies & Grammar Schools	No. of Scholars	Primary and Common Schools	No. of Scholars	No. of Scholars at public charge
John B Wright											
George F Wright											
Rite Wright											
George W Wright											
George A Wright											
Joseph Wright											
Elizabeth Wright											
Wm Wright											
John Wright											

Names of Heads of Families [Continued from prior page]	No. of white persons over 90 years of age in each family who cannot read or write	Identification
John B Wright		1896 John B. Wright of Franklin County, son of 1823 James Wright of Franklin County, grandson of 1809 William Wright of Franklin County, and probably great grandson of 1792 John Wright of Fauquier County
George F Wright		George Finney Wright, son of 1830 William Wright of Franklin County, grandson of 1809 William Wright of Franklin County, and probably great grandson of 1792 John Wright of Fauquier County
Rite Wright		1855 Wright Wright of Franklin County, son of 1815 Joseph Wright of Bedford County and grandson of 1763 Thomas Wright of Bedford County
George W Wright		George Washington Wright, son of 1843 George Wright of Franklin County, grandson of 1809 William Wright of Franklin County, and probably great grandson of 1792 John Wright of Fauquier County
George A Wright		Probably George Wright, son of 1874 Ezekiel Wright of Franklin County, grandson of 1845 John Wright of Franklin County, probably great grandson of 1809 William Wright of Franklin County, and great great grandson of 1792 John Wright of Fauquier County
Joseph Wright		Joseph Kemp Wright, son of 1855 Wright Wright of Franklin County, grandson of 1815 Joseph Wright of Bedford County, and great grandson of 1763 Thomas Wright of Bedford County
Elizabeth Wright		Elizabeth (Abshire) Wright, widow of 1839 John A. Wright of Franklin County, a son of 1830 William Wright of Franklin County, grandson of 1809 William Wright of Franklin County, and probably great grandson of 1792 John Wright of Fauquier County
Wm Wright		
John Wright		1845 John Wright of Franklin County, probably son of 1809 William Wright of Franklin County and grandson of 1792 John Wright of Fauquier County

Appendix: Franklin County, Virginia, 1840 Census

| Names of Heads of Families | Free White Persons (including heads of families) | | | | | | | | | | | | | |
| | Males | | | | | | | | | | | | | |
	Under 5	5 & under 10	10 & under 15	15 & under 20	20 & under 30	30 & under 40	40 & under 50	50 & under 60	60 & under 70	70 & under 80	80 & under 90	90 & under 100	100 and upwards
Thos Wright	1	0	0	1	0	0	0	0	0	0	1	0	0
James Wright	2	2	1	0	0	0	0	1	0	0	0	0	0

Names of Heads of Families [Continued from prior page]	Under 5	5 & under 10	10 & under 15	15 & under 20	20 & under 30	30 & under 40	40 & under 50	50 & under 60	60 & under 70	70 & under 80	80 & under 90	90 & under 100	100 and upwards
					Free White Persons (including heads of families) [Continued]								
					Females								
Thos Wright	0	0	0	0	1	0	0	1	0	0	0	0	0
James Wright	0	1	1	2	0	0	1	0	0	0	0	0	0

Appendix: Franklin County, Virginia, 1840 Census

		Free Colored Persons										
		Males						Females				
Names of Heads of Families [Continued from prior page]	Under 10	10 & under 24	24 & under 36	36 & under 55	55 & under 100	100 & and upwards	5 & under 10	10 & under 24	24 & under 36	36 & under 55	55 & under 100	100 and upwards
Thos Wright												
James Wright												

Appendix: Franklin County, Virginia, 1840 Census

					Slaves								
	Males						Females						
Names of Heads of Families [Continued from prior page]	Under 10	10 & under 24	24 & under 36	36 & under 55	55 & under 100	100 and upwards	Under 10	10 & under 24	24 & under 36	36 & under 55	55 & under 100	100 and upwards	Total
Thos Wright	1	1	2	0	0	0	1	1	1	0	1	0	13
James Wright	0	2	0	0	0	0	2	0	1	0	0	0	16

Appendix: Franklin County, Virginia, 1840 Census

Names of Heads of Families [Continued from prior page]	Mining	Agri-culture	Commerce	Manu-facture and trades	Navi-gation of the ocean	Navi-gation of canals lakes and rivers	Learned profes-sions and engineers	Pensioners for Revolutionary or Military Ser-vices Included in the foregoing Names	Ages	Under 14	14 & under 25	25 and upwards	Blind	Insane and idiots at public charge	Insane and idiots at private charge
							Number of Persons in each Family Employed in					**Deaf and Dumb, Blind and Insane White Persons Included in the Foregoing**				
										Deaf and Dumb				Insane and Idiots	
Thos Wright		7													
James Wright		6													

Appendix: Franklin County, Virginia, 1840 Census

| Names of Heads of Families [Continued from prior page] | Deaf and Dumb, Blind and Insane Colored Persons Included in the Foregoing | | | | Schools, &c. | | | | | | |
| | Deaf, Dumb, and Blind | | Insane and Idiots | | | | | | | | |
	Deaf & Dumb	Blind	Insane and idiots at private charge	Insane and idiots at public charge	Univer-sities or College	Number of Students	Acade-mies & Grammar Schools	No. of Scholars	Primary and Common Schools	No. of Scholars	No. of Scholars at public charge
Thos Wright											
James Wright											

Appendix: Franklin County, Virginia, 1840 Census

Names of Heads of Families [Continued from prior page]	No. of white persons over 90 years of age in each family who cannot read or write	Identification
Thos Wright		1849 Thomas Wright of Franklin County, son of 1815 Joseph Wright of Bedford County, and grandson of 1763 Thomas Wright of Bedford County
James Wright		1857 James Wright of Delaware County, Indiana, son of 1830 William Wright of Franklin County, grandson of 1809 William Wright of Franklin County, and probably great grandson of 1792 John Wright of Fauquier County

1850 CENSUS

FRANKLIN COUNTY, VIRGINIA

Appendix: Franklin County, Virginia, 1850 Census

Name	Age	Sex	Color	Occupation	Value of Real Estate	Place of Birth	Married Within Year	Attended School Within Year	Cannot Read & Write	Deaf Dumb Blind Insane etc.	Identification
254/254 08/24/1850											
[Green Pinckard School]											
Susan Wright	9	F				Virginia					
327/326 08/29/1850											
Ansalom Wright	45	M		Blacksmith	$500	Virginia					1883 Anslem Wright of Franklin County, son of William Wright
William Wright	23	M		Laborer		Virginia					
Abraham Wright	21	M		Laborer		Virginia					
Letitia Wright	19	F				Virginia					
Mary Wright	17	F				Virginia					
Sarah Wright	15	F				Virginia					
Charlotte Wright	13	F				Virginia					
Andrew Wright	11	M				Virginia					
Louisa Wright	9	F				Virginia					
Oliver Wright	7	M				Virginia					
Tazwell Wright	6	M				Virginia					
James Wright	4	M				Virginia					
484/482 09/15/1850											
John A. Wright	32	M		Farmer	$2500	Virginia					1905 John A. Wright of Franklin County, son of
Mary E Wright	21	F				Virginia					1843 George Wright of Franklin County,
George C. Wright	3	M				Virginia					grandson of 1809 William Wright of Franklin
Mary Wright	80	F				Virginia					County, and probably great grandson of 1792 John Wright of Fauquier County

Appendix: Franklin County, Virginia, 1850 Census

Name	Age	Sex	Color	Occupation	Value of Real Estate	Place of Birth	Married Within Year	Attended School Within Year	Cannot Read & Write	Deaf Dumb Blind Insane etc.	Identification
609/606 09/27/1850											
Joseph K. Wright	40	M		Farmer	$350	Virginia					Joseph Kemp Wright, son of 1855 Wright
Sarah Wright	39	F				Virginia					Wright of Franklin County, grandson of 1815 Joseph Wright of Bedford County, and great grandson of 1763 Thomas Wright of Bedford County
691/688 10/03/1850											
Robert P. Wright	28	M		Farmer	$1500	Virginia					1890 Robert Penn Wright of Franklin County,
Rhoda Wright	30	F				Virginia					son of 1849 Thomas Wright of Franklin
William T. Wright	10	M				Virginia					County, grandson of 1815 Joseph Wright of
Susannah R. Wright	8	F				Virginia					Bedford County, and great grandson of 1763
John R. Wright	6	M				Virginia					Thomas Wright of Bedford County
Laurence M. Wright	4	M				Virginia					
_____ Wright	1	M				Virginia					
Susannah Wright	60	F				Virginia					
753/750 10/06/1850											
Right Wright	70	M		Farmer	$3000	Virginia					1855 Wright Wright of Franklin County, son of
Mary Wright	60	F				Virginia					1815 Joseph Wright of Bedford County and
Jane Wright	40	F				Virginia					grandson of 1763 Thomas Wright of Bedford
Fleming J. T. Wright	28	M				Virginia					County
Mary A. Wright	20	F				Virginia					

Appendix: Franklin County, Virginia, 1850 Census

Name	Age	Sex	Color	Occupation	Value of Real Estate	Place of Birth	Married Within Year	Attended School Within Year	Cannot Read & Write	Deaf Dumb Blind Insane etc.	Identification

787/784 10/08/1850

Name	Age	Sex	Color	Occupation	Value of Real Estate	Place of Birth	Married Within Year	Attended School Within Year	Cannot Read & Write	Deaf Dumb Blind Insane etc.	Identification
George W. Wright	47	M		Farmer	$150	Virginia					George Washington Wright, son of 1843 George
Mary [Abshire]	40	F				Virginia					Wright of Franklin County, grandson of 1809
Quintina Wright	22	F				Virginia					William Wright of Franklin County, and probably
Elliott Wright	20	M				Virginia					great grandson of 1792 John Wright of Fauquier
George Wright	17	M				Virginia					County
Sarah K. Wright	16	F				Virginia					
Elizabeth Wright	14	F				Virginia					
Charlotte Wright	12	F				Virginia					
Julia Wright	10	F				Virginia					
James M. Wright	6	M				Virginia					
Susan E. Wright	3	F				Virginia					

792/789 10/09/1850

Name	Age	Sex	Color	Occupation	Value of Real Estate	Place of Birth	Married Within Year	Attended School Within Year	Cannot Read & Write	Deaf Dumb Blind Insane etc.	Identification
George F. Wright	65	M		Farmer	$2000	Virginia					George Finney Wright, son of 1830 William
Ammon Wright	36	M				Virginia					Wright of Franklin County, grandson of 1809
											William Wright of Franklin County, and probably
											great grandson of 1792 John Wright of Fauquier
											County

794/791 10/09/1850

Name	Age	Sex	Color	Occupation	Value of Real Estate	Place of Birth	Married Within Year	Attended School Within Year	Cannot Read & Write	Deaf Dumb Blind Insane etc.	Identification
Skelton Wright	45	M		Farmer	$210	Virginia					Skelton Wright, son of 1839 John A. Wright of
Joana Wright	27	F				Virginia					Franklin County, grandson of 1830 William
Cynthia Wright	11	F				Virginia					Wright of Franklin County, great grandson
William Wright	9	M				Virginia					of 1809 William Wright of Franklin County, and
John Wright	7	M				Virginia					probably great great grandson of 1792 John
Elizabeth Wright	4	F				Virginia					Wright of Fauquier County
Sarah Wright	1	F				Virginia					

Appendix: Franklin County, Virginia, 1850 Census

Name	Age	Sex	Color	Occupation	Value of Real Estate	Place of Birth	Married Within Year	Attended School Within Year	Cannot Read & Write	Deaf Dumb Blind Insane etc.	Identification
815/812 10/10/1850											
Jacob Bowles	44	M		Laborer		Virginia					Mary "Polly" (Wright) Bowles, daughter of 1843 George Wright of Franklin County, grand-daughter of 1809 William Wright of Franklin County, and probably great granddaughter of 1792 John Wright of Fauquier County
Mary Wright	41	F				Virginia					
Christina Bowles	18	F				Virginia					
William Bowles	15	M				Virginia					
Lucy Bowles	13	F				Virginia					
Cynthia Bowles	12	F				Virginia					
Mary Bowles	8	F				Virginia					
816/813 10/10/1850											
George Wright	50	M		Farmer	$2070	Virginia					George Washington Wright, son of 1843 George Wright of Franklin County, grandson of 1809 William Wright of Franklin County, and probably great grandson of 1792 John Wright of Fauquier County (listed twice apparently)
Mary Wright	45	F				Virginia					
Elizabeth Wright	14	F				Virginia					
Charlotte Wright	8	F				Virginia					
Julia Wright	6	F				Virginia					
James Wright	5	M				Virginia					
Susan Wright	3	F				Virginia					
823/820 10/10/1850											
Asa Wright	32	M		Farmer	$500	Virginia					1901 Asa Wright of Franklin County, son of 1839 John A. Wright of Franklin County, grandson of 1830 William Wright of Franklin County, great grandson of 1809 William Wright of Franklin County, and probably great great grandson of 1792 John Wright of Fauquier County
Mary Wright	22	F				Virginia					
Andrew Nunnerly	26	M		Laborer		Virginia					

Appendix: Franklin County, Virginia, 1850 Census

Name	Age	Sex	Color	Occupation	Value of Real Estate	Place of Birth	Married Within Year	Attended School Within Year	Cannot Read & Write	Deaf Dumb Blind Insane etc.	Identification
856/853 10/11/1850											
Elizabeth Wright	60	F		Farmer	$500	Virginia					Elizabeth (Abshire) Wright, widow of 1839
John Wright	25	M				Virginia					John A. Wright of Franklin County, a son of 1830 William Wright of Franklin County, grandson of 1809 William Wright of Franklin County, and probably great grandson of 1792 John Wright of Fauquier County
858/855 10/11/1850											
William Wright	25	M		Farmer	$150	Virginia					William H. Wright, son of 1839 John A. Wright
Ann Wright	26	F				Virginia					of Franklin County, grandson of 1830 William Wright of Franklin County, great grandson of 1809 William Wright of Franklin County, and probably great great grandson of 1792 John Wright of Fauquier County
978/974 10/19/1850											
Ezekiel Wright	64	M		Farmer	$500	Virginia					1874 Ezekiel Wright of Franklin County, son of
Elizabeth Wright	62	F				Virginia					1845 John Wright of Franklin County, probably
Teresa Wright	27	F				Virginia					grandson of 1809 William Wright of Franklin
Susan Wright	25	F				Virginia					County, and great grandson of 1792 John
Mary Wright	23	F				Virginia					Wright of Fauquier County
William Wright	15	M				Virginia					
Sparrel Forbes	26	M		Laborer		Virginia					

Appendix: Franklin County, Virginia, 1850 Census

Name	Age	Sex	Color	Occupation	Value of Real Estate	Place of Birth	Married Within Year	Attended School Within Year	Cannot Read & Write	Deaf Dumb Blind Insane etc.	Identification

986/982 10/19/1850

Name	Age	Sex	Color	Occupation	Value of Real Estate	Place of Birth	Married Within Year	Attended School Within Year	Cannot Read & Write	Deaf Dumb Blind Insane etc.	Identification
John B. Wright	42	M		Farmer	$150	Virginia					1896 John B. Wright of Franklin County, son
Jemima Wright	46	F				Virginia					of 1823 James Wright of Franklin County,
Nancy Wright	21	F				Virginia					grandson of 1809 William Wright of Franklin
James Wright	18	M				Virginia					County, and probably great grandson of 1792
Abraham Wright	16	M				Virginia					John Wright of Fauquier County
Robert Wright	14	M				Virginia					
Margaret Wright	12	F				Virginia					
William Wright	9	M				Virginia					
George Wright	2	M				Virginia					

1003/999 10/19/1850

Name	Age	Sex	Color	Occupation	Value of Real Estate	Place of Birth	Married Within Year	Attended School Within Year	Cannot Read & Write	Deaf Dumb Blind Insane etc.	Identification
James G. Wright	50	M		Farmer	$150	Virginia					James Grant Wright, son of 1823 James Wright
Ann Wright	45	F				Virginia					of Franklin County, grandson of 1809 William
James G. Wright	14	M				Virginia					Wright of Franklin County, and probably great
Anthony Wright	13	M				Virginia					grandson of 1792 John Wright of Fauquier
Pamelia Wright	7	F				Virginia					County
Margaret Wright	10	F				Virginia					

1015/1011 10/21/1850

Name	Age	Sex	Color	Occupation	Value of Real Estate	Place of Birth	Married Within Year	Attended School Within Year	Cannot Read & Write	Deaf Dumb Blind Insane etc.	Identification
Margaret Wright	84	F				Virginia					Margaret "Peggy" (Young) Wright, widow of
Mary Wright	50	F				Virginia					1823 James Wright of Franklin County, a son of 1809 William Wright of Franklin County and probably grandson of 1792 John Wright of Fauquier County

Appendix: Franklin County, Virginia, 1850 Census

Name	Age	Sex	Color	Occupation	Value of Real Estate	Place of Birth	Married Within Year	Attended School Within Year	Cannot Read & Write	Deaf Dumb Blind Insane etc.	Identification

1026/1022 10/22/1850

Name	Age	Sex	Color	Occupation	Value of Real Estate	Place of Birth	Married Within Year	Attended School Within Year	Cannot Read & Write	Deaf Dumb Blind Insane etc.	Identification
Goodman A. Wright	37	M		Farmer	$100	Virginia					1886 Goodman A. Wright of Franklin County, Kansas, son of 1823 James Wright of Franklin County, grandson of 1809 William Wright of Franklin County, and probably great grandson of 1792 John Wright of Fauquier County
Elizabeth Wright	44	F				Virginia					
Catharine Wright	13	F				Virginia					
John Wright	11	M				Virginia					
Sarah Wright	7	F				Virginia					
Phoebe Wright	4	F				Virginia					
Samuel Wright	9/12	M				Virginia					

1049/1045 10/23/1850

Name	Age	Sex	Color	Occupation	Value of Real Estate	Place of Birth	Married Within Year	Attended School Within Year	Cannot Read & Write	Deaf Dumb Blind Insane etc.	Identification
Thomas F. Taylor	30	M		Farmer	$1500	Virginia					Sarah (Greer) Wright, the widow of 1845 William Wright of Franklin County, a son of 1830 William Wright of Franklin County, grandson of 1809 William Wright of Franklin County, and probably great grandson of 1792 John Wright of Fauquier County
Ann C. Taylor	22	F				Virginia					
Henrietta Taylor	2	F				Virginia					
_____ Taylor	5/12	M				Virginia					
Sarah Wright	40	F				Virginia					
Susan Wright	8	F				Virginia					

1514/1508 11/21/1850

Name	Age	Sex	Color	Occupation	Value of Real Estate	Place of Birth	Married Within Year	Attended School Within Year	Cannot Read & Write	Deaf Dumb Blind Insane etc.	Identification
Joseph Wright	50	M		Blacksmith		Virginia					Joseph Wright, son of 1845 John Wright of Franklin County, probably grandson of 1809 William Wright of Franklin County, and great grandson of 1792 John Wright of Fauquier County
Judith Wright	54	F				Virginia					

Dated January 10, 1851

Total 11,704 persons

Appendix: Franklin County, Virginia, 1860 Census

Name	Age	Sex	Color	Occupation	Value of Real Estate	Value of Personal Property	Place of Birth	Married Within Year	Attended School Within Year	Cannot Read & Write	Deaf Dumb Blind Insane etc.	Identification
SW District												
505/500 07/26/1860												
Jas G. Wright, Jr.	26	M		Blacksmith		60						James Grant Wright, Jr., son of
Jane Wright	30	F								1		James Grant Wright, grandson
James W. Wright	6	M										of 1823 James Wright of
Randolph A. Wright	3	M										Franklin County, great grandson
												of 1809 William Wright of
												Franklin County, and probably
												great great grandson of 1792
												John Wright of Fauquier County
SW District												
1269/1268 10/04/1860												
Ezekiel Wright	75	M		Farmer						1		1874 Ezekiel Wright of Franklin
Elizabeth Wright	79	F								1		County, son of 1845 John
Tece Wright	40	F			500	200				1		Wright of Franklin County,
Susan Wright	37	F								1		probably son of 1809 William
William Minnix	23	M										Wright of Franklin County, and
												great grandson of 1792 John
												Wright of Fauquier County
SW District												
1282/1281 10/04/1860												
Margt Wright	95	F								1		Margaret "Peggy" (Young)
Mary Wright	62	F								1		Wright, widow of 1823 James
												Wright of Franklin County, a
												son of 1809 William Wright of
												Franklin County and probably
												grandson of 1792 John Wright
												of Fauquier County

Appendix: Franklin County, Virginia, 1860 Census

Name	Age	Sex	Color	Occupation	Value of Real Estate	Value of Personal Property	Place of Birth	Married Within Year	Attended School Within Year	Cannot Read & Write	Deaf Dumb Blind Insane etc.	Identification
SW District												
1334/1334 10/12/1860												
Jno B. Wright	53	M		Farmer						1		1896 John B. Wright of Franklin
Jemima Wright	56	F								1		County, son of 1823 James
Abram Wright	25	M			400							Wright of Franklin County,
Wm Wright	15	M										grandson of 1809 William
Geo Wright	11	M										Wright of Franklin County, and
Mahala Mason	35	F										probably great grandson of
Nancy Mason	3	F										1792 John Wright of Fauquier
												County
SW District												
1335/1335 10/12/1860												
James Wright	27	M		Farmer		50	Va	1				1905 James G. Wright of
Mary Wright	22	F					Va	1				Franklin County, son of 1896
												John B. Wright of Franklin
												County, grandson of 1823
												James Wright of Franklin
												County, great grandson of 1809
												William Wright of Franklin
												County, and probably great
												great grandson of 1792 John
												Wright of Fauquier County

Appendix: Franklin County, Virginia, 1860 Census

Name	Age	Sex	Color	Occupation	Value of Real Estate	Value of Personal Property	Place of Birth	Married Within Year	Attended School Within Year	Cannot Read & Write	Deaf Dumb Blind Insane etc.	Identification
Union Hall District 301/295 07/11/1860												
Abram O. Wright	27	M		Farmer		35	Va					1862 Abraham O. Wright of
Elizabeth Wright	27	F					Va					Franklin County, son of 1883
John W. Wright	7	M					Va					Anslem Wright of Franklin
Victoria A. Wright	5	F					Va					County and grandson of William
Willson A. Wright	1	M					Va					Wright
Union Hall District 349/339 07/14/1860												
Ansom Wright	55	M		Blacksmith		100	Va					1883 Anslem Wright of Franklin
Sarah A. Wright	25	F					Va					County, son of William Wright
Louisa Wright	20	F					Va					
Oliver T. Wright	19	M					Va					
Jas Wright	13	M					Va					
Wm R. Wright	33	M		Farmer	950	300	Va					
S.L.T. Wright	2	M					Va					
Gills Creek District 408/392 07/19/1860												
Jesse Bradley	34	M		Farmer	1050	2714	Va					1923 Tazwell M. Wright of
Drucilla Bradley	26	F					Va					Bedford County, son of 1883
Silas T Bradley	7	M					Va					Aslem Wright of Franklin County
Mary Bradley	2	F					Va					and grandson of William Wright
Tazwell M. Wright	16	M					Va					

Name	Age	Sex	Color	Occupation	Value of Real Estate	Value of Personal Property	Place of Birth	Married Within Year	Attended School Within Year	Cannot Read & Write	Deaf Dumb Blind Insane etc.	Identification
Hales Ford District **513/496 07/25/1860**												
Jas Wright	64	M		Farmer	5000	12,068						1877 James Wright of Franklin County, son of 1850 Tommey Wright of Bedford County, grandson of 1803 John Wright of Bedford County, and great grandson of 1763 Thomas Wright of Bedford County
Judith P. Wright	43	F										
James E. M. Wright	12	M							1			
Thos H. Wright	7	M							1			
O.R.F.H. Wright	3	F										
Hales Ford District **617/596 08/01/1860**												
Edward Hall	76	M				75	Va			1		1869 Anthony K. Wright of Franklin County, son of James Grant Wright, grandson of 1823 James Wright of Franklin County, great grandson of 1809 William Wright of Franklin County, and probably great great grandson of 1792 John Wright of Fauquier County
Rebecca Hall	67	F					Va			1		
Anthoney Wright	22	M					Va					
Alean Wright	22	F					Va			1		

Appendix: Franklin County, Virginia, 1860 Census

Name	Age	Sex	Color	Occupation	Value of Real Estate	Value of Personal Property	Place of Birth	Married Within Year	Attended School Within Year	Cannot Read & Write	Deaf Dumb Blind Insane etc.	Identification
Rocky Mount 620/599 08/01/1860												
Crockett A. Wright	34	M		Farm Laborer			Va			1		1901 Crockett Anderson Wright
Elizabeth Wright	34	F					Va			1		of Franklin County, son of Smith
Jas Wright	13	M					Va		1			Wright (Montgomery County)
Isaac Wright	11	M					Va		1			
David Wright	9	M					Va		1			
Harriett Wright	8	F					Va		1			
John H. Wright	7	M					Va					
Sersena Wright	5	F					Va					
Wm C. Wright	1	M					Va					
Gogginsville 759/735 08/08/1860												
John A. Wright	42	M		Constable	1250	5531	Va					1905 John A. Wright of Franklin
Mary E. Wright	31	F					Va					County, son of 1843 George
Charles C. Wright	9	M					Va			1		Wright of Franklin County,
John M. Wright	7	M					Va			1		grandson of 1809 William Wright of Franklin County, and probably great grandson of 1792 John Wright of Fauquier County

Appendix: Franklin County, Virginia, 1860 Census

Name	Age	Sex	Color	Occupation	Value of Real Estate	Value of Personal Property	Place of Birth	Married Within Year	Attended School Within Year	Cannot Read & Write	Deaf Dumb Blind Insane etc.	Identification
Bonbrook District **765/740 08/03/1860**												
Otey Wright	32	M		Farmer		3045						1918 Otey Wright of Franklin County, son of 1839 John A. Wright of Franklin County, grandson of 1830 William Wright of Franklin County, great grandson of 1809 William Wright of Franklin County, and probably great great grandson of 1792 John Wright of Fauquier County
Caroline F. Wright	22	F										
Mary E. Wright	4	F										
Sallie A. Wright	2	F										
John O. Wright	5/12	M										
Elizabeth Wright	75	F								1		
Bonbrook District **882/859 08/21/1860**												
Asa Wright	44	M		Farmer	2000	3305	Va					1901 Asa Wright of Franklin County, son of 1839 John A. Wright of Franklin County, grandson of 1830 William Wright of Franklin County, great grandson of 1809 William Wright of Franklin County, and probably great great grandson of 1792 John Wright of Fauquier County
Mary Wright	30	F					Va					
Mary C. Showalter	6	F					Va					
Woodson Meador	16	M					Va			1		

Appendix: Franklin County, Virginia, 1860 Census

Name	Age	Sex	Color	Occupation	Value of Real Estate	Value of Personal Property	Place of Birth	Married Within Year	Attended School Within Year	Cannot Read & Write	Deaf Dumb Blind Insane etc.	Identification
Bonbrook District 883/860 08/21/1860												
William Wright	38	M		Farmer		80	Va			1		William H. Wright, son of 1839
Nancy Wright	38	F					Va					John A. Wright of Franklin
Jas Nunerly	11	M					Va					County, grandson of 1830
												William Wright of Franklin
												County, great grandson of 1809
												William Wright of Franklin
												County, and probably great
												great grandson of 1792 John
												Wright of Fauquier County
Boonsmill District 916/893 08/22/1860												
Geo F. Wright	74	M		Farmer	1250	200	Va					George Finney Wright, son of
Persilla Drewry	54	F					Va			1		1830 William Wright of Franklin
Sarah Guthrie	11	F					Va		1			County, grandson of 1809
												William Wright of Franklin
												County, and probably great
												grandson of 1792 John Wright
												of Fauquier County

Name	Age	Sex	Color	Occupation	Value of Real Estate	Value of Personal Property	Place of Birth	Married Within Year	Attended School Within Year	Cannot Read & Write	Deaf Dumb Blind Insane etc.	Identification
Cooper's Cove District **1022/1001 08/26/1860**												
Mary Wright	69	F			5000	1713	Va					Mary "Polly" (Scott) Wright, widow of 1855 Wright Wright of Franklin County, a son of 1815 Joseph Wright of Bedford County and grandson of 1763 Thomas Wright of Bedford County
F. J. T. Wright	39	M		Farmer		2000	Va					
Henry S. Wright	35	M		Farmer			Va					
Mary A. Wright	28	F					Va					
Cooper's Cove District **1051/1030 08/27/1860**												
John H. Booth	40	M		Farmer	2064	500	Va					Andrew J. Wright of Bedford County, son of 1883 Anslem Wright of Franklin County and grandson of William Wright
Nancy G. Booth	37	F					Va					
Araminta Booth	15	F					Va					
Mary J. Booth	13	F					Va					
Jesse L. Booth	11	M					Va					
Drucilla Booth	4	F					Va					
_____ Booth	2	M					Va					
Andrew J. Wright	23	M		Farm Laborer			Va			1		

Appendix: Franklin County, Virginia, 1860 Census

Name	Age	Sex	Color	Occupation	Value of Real Estate	Value of Personal Property	Place of Birth	Married Within Year	Attended School Within Year	Cannot Read & Write	Deaf Dumb Blind Insane etc.	Identification
Cooper's Cove District 1053/1032 08/27/1860												
Robt B. Wright	38	M		Farmer	10000	4100	Va					1890 Robert Penn Wright of
Rhoda Wright	40	F					Va					Franklin County, son of 1849
Wm T. Wright	19	M					Va					Thomas Wright of Franklin
John R. Wright	16	M					Va					County, grandson of 1815
Larance M. Wright	12	M					Va					Joseph Wright of Bedford
Henry S. Wright	10	M					Va					County, and great grandson of
Milton M. Wright	8	M					Va					1763 Thomas Wright of Bedford
Cicero A. Wright	4	M					Va					County
Nancy L. Wright	1	F					Va					
Hales Ford District 1117/1089 08/29/1860												
Joseph K. Wright	50	M		Farmer	1000	2165	Va					Joseph Kemp Wright, son of
Sarah R. Wright	49	F					Va					1855 Wright Wright of Franklin County, grandson of 1815 Joseph Wright of Bedford County, and great grandson of 1763 Thomas Wright of Bedford County

Names of Slave Owners	No of Slaves	Age	Sex	Color	Fugitives from the State	Number manumitted	Deaf & dumb, blind, insane, or idiotic	No. of Slave houses	Identification
John A. Wright	1	63	M	B					1905 John A. Wright of Franklin County, son of 1843 George Wright of Franklin County, grandson of 1809 William Wright of Franklin County, and probably great grandson of 1792 John Wright of Fauquier County
	1	23	M	B					
	1	23	F	B					
	1	8	M	B					
	1	5	M	B					
	1	2	M	B					
Otey Wright	1	24	F	B					1918 Otey Wright of Franklin County, son of 1839 John A. Wright of Franklin County, grandson of 1830 William Wright of Franklin County, great grandson of 1809 William Wright of Franklin County, and probably great great grandson of 1792 John Wright of Fauquier County
	1	6	M	B					
	1	2	M	B					
Elizabeth Wright	1	35	M	M					Elizabeth (Abshire) Wright, widow of 1839 John A. Wright of Franklin County, a son of 1830 William Wright of Franklin County, grandson of 1809 William Wright of Franklin County, and probably great grandson of 1792 John Wright of Fauquier County
Mary Wright	1	65	F	B					Mary "Polly" (Scott) Wright, widow of 1855 Wright Wright of Franklin County, a son of 1815 Joseph Wright of Bedford County and grandson of 1763 Thomas Wright of Bedford County
	1	57	F	B					

Appendix: Franklin County, Virginia, 1860 Census [Slave Schedules]

Names of Slave Owners	No of Slaves	Age	Sex	Color	Fugitives from the State	Number manumitted	Deaf & dumb, blind, insane, or idiotic	No. of Slave houses	Identification
Robt P. Wright	1	50	M	B					1890 Robert Penn Wright of Franklin County, son of 1849 Thomas Wright of Franklin County, grandson of 1815 Joseph Wright of Bedford County, and great grandson of 1763 Thomas Wright of Bedford County
	1	15	M	B					
	1	12	F	M					
	1	10	F	M					
	1	8	F	B					
Joseph K. Wright	1	63	F	B					Joseph Kemp Wright, son of 1855 Wright Wright of Franklin County, grandson of 1815 Joseph Wright of Bedford County, and great grandson of 1763 Thomas Wright of Bedford County
	1	30	M	B					

1870 CENSUS

FRANKLIN COUNTY, VIRGINIA

Appendix: Franklin County, Virginia, 1870 Census

Name	Age	Sex	Color	Occupation	Value of Real Estate	Value of Personal Property	Place of Birth	Married Within Year	Born Within Year	Attended School Within Year	Cannot Read	Cannot Write	Deaf Dumb Blind Insane or or Idiot

Bonbrook Township

071/071 06/30/1870

Name	Age	Sex	Color	Occupation	Value of Real Estate	Value of Personal Property	Place of Birth	Married Within Year	Born Within Year	Attended School Within Year	Cannot Read	Cannot Write	Deaf Dumb Blind Insane or or Idiot
John A. Wright	52	M	W	Farmer	2500	700	Virginia						
Mary Wright	40	F	W	Keeping House			Virginia						
George Wright	19	M	W	Farm Laborer			Virginia				1	1	
John Wright	18	M	W	Farm Laborer			Virginia						
Florena Lynch	5	F	W	Domes Servant			Virginia						

092/096 07/02/1870

Name	Age	Sex	Color	Occupation	Value of Real Estate	Value of Personal Property	Place of Birth	Married Within Year	Born Within Year	Attended School Within Year	Cannot Read	Cannot Write	Deaf Dumb Blind Insane or or Idiot
George Wright	85	M	W	Farmer	1000	100	Virginia						
Persilia Drewry	59	F	W	Keeps House			Virginia				1	1	
Turner(?) Drewry	30	F	W	Dom Servant			Virginia						
George Drewry	1	M	W				Virginia						

153/162 07/07/1870

Name	Age	Sex	Color	Occupation	Value of Real Estate	Value of Personal Property	Place of Birth	Married Within Year	Born Within Year	Attended School Within Year	Cannot Read	Cannot Write	Deaf Dumb Blind Insane or or Idiot
William Wright	47	M	W	Farm Laborer			Virginia				1	1	
Nancy Wright	46	F	W	Keeps House			Virginia				1	1	
Mary Nunally	16	F	W				Virginia						

184/190 07/12/1870

Name	Age	Sex	Color	Occupation	Value of Real Estate	Value of Personal Property	Place of Birth	Married Within Year	Born Within Year	Attended School Within Year	Cannot Read	Cannot Write	Deaf Dumb Blind Insane or or Idiot
Asa Wright	55	M	W	Farmer	1500	500	Virginia						
Mary Wright	47	F	W	Keeping House			Virginia						
Mary Showalter	16	F	W	Without Occuptn			Virginia						
Saml Lavinder	12	M	W	Farm Laborer			Virginia						

Appendix: Franklin County, Virginia, 1870 Census

Name [Continued from prior page]	Male Citizen Over 21	Male Citizen Over 21 Without Right to Vote	Identification
Bonbrook Township			
071/071 06/20/1870			
John A. Wright Mary Wright George Wright John Wright Florena Lynch	1		1905 John A. Wright of Franklin County, son of 1843 George Wright of Franklin County, grandson of 1809 William Wright of Franklin County, and probably great grandson of 1792 John Wright of Fauquier County
092/096 07/02/1870			
George Wright Persilia Drewry Turner(?) Drewry George Drewry	1		George Finney Wright, son of 1830 William Wright of Franklin County, grandson of 1809 William Wright of Franklin County, and probably great grandson of 1792 John Wright of Fauquier County
153/162 07/07/1870			
William Wright Nancy Wright Mary Nunally	1		William H. Wright, son of 1839 John A. Wright of Franklin County, grandson of 1830 William Wright of Franklin County, great grandson of 1809 William Wright of Franklin County, and probably great great grandson of 1792 John Wright of Fauquier County
186/190 07/12/1870			
Asa Wright Mary Wright Mary Showalter Saul Lavinder	1		1901 Asa Wright of Franklin County, son of 1839 John A. Wright of Franklin County, grandson of 1830 William Wright of Franklin County, great grandson of 1809 William Wright of Franklin County, and probably great great grandson of 1792 John Wright of Fauquier County

Name	Age	Sex	Color	Occupation	Value of Real Estate	Value of Personal Property	Place of Birth	Married Within Year	Born Within Year	Attended School Within Year	Cannot Read	Cannot Write	Deaf Dumb Blind Insane or or Idiot
231/243 07/18/1870													
Wesley Wright	26	M	B	Farm Laborer			Virginia				1	1	
Katharine Wright	22	F	B	Keeps House			Virginia				1	1	
James Wright	3	M	B				Virginia						
John Wright	1	M	B				Virginia						
Virginia Wright	2/12	F	B				Virginia			Apl			
237/249 07/18/1870													
Joshua Wright	48	M	B	Farm Laborer		100	Virginia				1	1	
Julia Wright	45	F	B	Keeps House			Virginia				1	1	
249/261 07/19/1870													
Albert Kingery	53	M	W	Farmer		100	Virginia				1	1	
Ursula Kingery	50	F	W	Keeps House			Virginia					1	
Isaac Kingery	23	M	W	Farm Laborer			Virginia				1	1	
John Kingery	20	M	W	Farm Laborer			Virginia				1	1	
Susan Kingery	27	F	W	Farm Laborer			Virginia				1	1	
Nancy Kingery	15	F	W	Farm Laborer			Virginia				1	1	
Martha Kingery	14	F	W	Farm Laborer			Virginia				1	1	
Thomas Kingery	11	M	W	Farm Laborer			Virginia						
Katherine Kingery	9	F	W				Virginia						
Ursula Wright	2	F	W				Virginia						

Appendix: Franklin County, Virginia, 1870 Census

Name [Continued from prior page]	Male Citizen Over 21	Male Citizen Over 21 Without Right to Vote	Identification
231/263 07/18/1870			
Wesley Wright	1		John Wesley Wright, son of Joshua Wright
Katharine Wright			
James Wright			
John Wright			
Virginia Wright			
237/249 07/18/1870			
Joshua Wright	1		
Julia Wright			
249/261 07/19/1870			
Albert Kingery	1		Ursula Wright, daughter of Susan Wright, granddaughter of Ursley (Wright) Kingery, great
Ursula Kingery			granddaughter of Jane (Wright) Arthur, great great granddaughter of 1823 James Wright of
Isaac Kingery	1		Franklin County, great great great granddaughter of 1809 William Wright of Franklin County,
John Kingery			and probably great great great great granddaughter of 1792 John Wright of Fauquier County
Susan Kingery			
Nancy Kingery			
Martha Kingery			
Thomas Kingery			
Katherine Kingery			
Ursula Wright			

Name	Age	Sex	Color	Occupation	Value of Real Estate	Value of Personal Property	Place of Birth	Married Within Year	Born Within Year	Attended School Within Year	Cannot Read	Cannot Write	Deaf Dumb Blind Insane or or Idiot
330/342 07/25/1870													
Robert P. Wright	48	M	W	Farmer	800	800	Virginia						
Rhoda Wright	42	F	W	Keeping House			Virginia						
Lawrence Wright	22	M	W	Farm Laborer			Virginia						
Henry Wright	20	M	W	Farm Laborer			Virginia						
Milton Wright	17	M	W	Farm Laborer			Virginia						
Cicero Wright	14	M	W	Farm Laborer			Virginia						
Nancy Wright	10	F	W				Virginia						
Colman Arthur	19	M	W	Farm Laborer			Virginia						
337/349 07/25/1870													
Pleasant Wright	48	M	M	Miller		100	Virginia				1	1	
Aggy Wright	42	F	M	Keeping House			Virginia				1	1	
Manassa Wright	8	F	M				Virginia						
Maria Wright	6	F	M				Virginia						
Robert Wright	4	M	M				Virginia						
Fletcher Wright	1	M	M				Virginia						
359/371 07/26/1870													
William Wright	33	M	W	Farmer	1000	300	Virginia						
Octavia Wright	26	F	W	Keeping House			Virginia						
Florence Wright	7	F	W				Virginia						
John Wright	4	M	W				Virginia						
Henrietta Wright	2	F	W				Virginia						

Appendix: Franklin County, Virginia, 1870 Census

Name [Continued from prior page]	Male Citizen Over 21	Male Citizen Over 21 Without Right to Vote	Identification
330/342 07/25/1870			
Robert P. Wright	1		1890 Robert Penn Wright of Franklin County, son of 1849 Thomas Wright of Franklin County,
Rhoda Wright			grandson of 1815 Joseph Wright of Bedford County, and great grandson of 1763 Thomas
Lawrence Wright	1		Wright of Bedford County
Henry Wright			
Milton Wright			
Cicero Wright			
Nancy Wright			
Colman Arthur			
337/349 07/25/1870			
Pleasant Wright	1		1898 Pleasant Wright of Franklin County
Aggy Wright			
Manassa Wright			
Maria Wright			
Robert Wright			
Fletcher Wright			
359/371 07/26/1870			
William Wright	1		1928 William Thomas Wright of Roanoke County, son of 1890 Robert Penn Wright of Franklin
Octavia Wright			County, grandson of 1849 Thomas Wright of Franklin County, great grandson of 1815 Joseph
Florence Wright			Wright of Bedford County and great grandson of 1803 John Wright of Bedford County, and
John Wright			great great grandson of 1763 Thomas Wright of Bedford County
Henrietta Wright			

Appendix: Franklin County, Virginia, 1870 Census

Name	Age	Sex	Color	Occupation	Value of Real Estate	Value of Personal Property	Place of Birth	Married Within Year	Born Within Year	Attended School Within Year	Cannot Read	Cannot Write	Deaf Dumb Blind Insane or or Idiot
Gills Creek Township													
358/359 08/12/1870													
Andrew Wright	32	M	W	Farm Laborer			Virginia				1	1	
Sarah Wright	25	F	W	Keeps House			Virginia				1	1	
Obadiah Wright	4	M	W				Virginia						
399/400 08/13/1870													
Matthew R. Allen	55	M	W	Farmer	800	3000	Virginia						
Margaret Allen	36	F	W	Keeps House			Virginia						
Jennie Allen	11	F	W				Virginia						
William Allen	9	M	W				Virginia						
Matthew Allen	7	M	W				Virginia						
Mary Allen	6	F	W				Virginia						
Sallie Allen	3	F	W				Virginia						
Ellen Allen	1	F	W				Virginia						
James Wright	28	M	W	Farm Laborer			Virginia				1	1	
Edward Meador	18	M	W	Farm Laborer			Virginia				1	1	
Abram Allen	22	M	B	Farm Laborer			Virginia				1	1	
Wash English	16	M	B	Farm Laborer			Virginia				1	1	
Martha Allen	18	F	M	Cook			Virginia				1	1	
Long Branch Township													
293/293 09/06/1870													
Sarah Wright	43	F	W	Housekeeping			Virginia					1	
Martha Wright	21	F	W	at home			Virginia					1	
John Wright	18	M	W	" labor			Virginia				1	1	

Appendix: Franklin County, Virginia, 1870 Census

Name [Continued from prior page]	Male Citizen Over 21	Male Citizen Over 21 Without Right to Vote	Identification
Gills Creek Township			
358/359 08/12/1870			
Andrew Wright	1		Andrew J. Wright of Bedford County, son of 1883 Anslem Wright of Franklin County and grandson of William Wright
Sarah Wright			
Obadiah Wright			
399/400 08/13/1870			
Matthew R. Allen	1		
Margaret Allen			
Jennie Allen			
William Allen			
Matthew Allen			
Mary Allen			
Sallie Allen			
Ellen Allen			
James Wright	1		
Edward Meador			
Abram Allen			
Wash English			
Martha Allen			
Long Branch Township			
293/293 09/06/1870			
Sarah Wright			
Martha Wright			
John Wright			

Appendix: Franklin County, Virginia, 1870 Census

Name	Age	Sex	Color	Occupation	Value of Real Estate	Value of Personal Property	Place of Birth	Married Within Year	Born Within Year	Attended School Within Year	Cannot Read	Cannot Write	Deaf Dumb Blind Insane or or Idiot

Maggodee Township

186/181 09/31/1870

Name	Age	Sex	Color	Occupation	Value of Real Estate	Value of Personal Property	Place of Birth	Married Within Year	Born Within Year	Attended School Within Year	Cannot Read	Cannot Write	Deaf Dumb Blind Insane or or Idiot
Sparrell Forbs	48	M	W	Farmer		100	Virginia						
Elizabeth Forbs	14	F	W	Keeping house			Virginia						
Mary Forbs	11	F	M				Virginia						
Sparrell Forbs	7	M	M				Virginia						
Ezekiel Wright	86	M	W				Virginia				1	1	
Tesey Wright	47	F	W				Virginia				1	1	
Susan Wright	44	F	W				Virginia				1	1	
John Webster	51	M	W	Farmer	1200	800	Virginia				1	1	

171/176 10/04/1870

Name	Age	Sex	Color	Occupation	Value of Real Estate	Value of Personal Property	Place of Birth	Married Within Year	Born Within Year	Attended School Within Year	Cannot Read	Cannot Write	Deaf Dumb Blind Insane or or Idiot
John Neall	47	M	W	Farmer		100	Virginia				1	1	
Claire Neall	33	F	W	Keeping house			Virginia				1	1	
Emily Grifasen	60	F	W	Keeping house			Virginia				1	1	
William Grifasen	20	M	W	Farm Laborer			Virginia		May				
Samuel Whorley	19	M	W	Farm Laborer			Virginia		Sept		1	1	
Ayliss Whorley	17	F	W	Keeping house			Virginia				1	1	
James Wright	6	M	W				Virginia						

180/185 10/04/1870

Name	Age	Sex	Color	Occupation	Value of Real Estate	Value of Personal Property	Place of Birth	Married Within Year	Born Within Year	Attended School Within Year	Cannot Read	Cannot Write	Deaf Dumb Blind Insane or or Idiot
Josiah Wright	61	M	B	Farm Laborer			Virginia				1	1	
Charlotte Wright	55	F	B	Keeping house			Virginia				1	1	
Kiery Wright	19	M	B	Farm Laborer			Virginia				1	1	
Brir Wright	18	F	B	Farm Laborer			Virginia				1	1	

Appendix: Franklin County, Virginia, 1870 Census

Name [Continued from prior page]	Male Citizen Over 21	Male Citizen Over 21 Without Right to Vote	Identification

<u>Maggodee Township</u>

186/181 09/31/1870

Sparrell Forbs	1		1874 Ezekiel Wright of Franklin County, son of 1845 John Wright of Franklin County, probably grandson of 1809 William Wright of Franklin County, and great grandson of 1792 John Wright of Fauquier County
Elizabeth Forbs			
Mary Forbs			
Sparrell Forbs			
Ezekiel Wright	1		
Tesey Wright			
Susan Wright			
John Webster	1		

171/176 10/04/1870

John Neall	1	
Claire Neall		
Emily Grifasen		
William Grifasen		
Samuel Whorley		
Ayliss Whorley		
James Wright		

180/185 10/04/1870

Josiah Wright	1	
Charlotte Wright		
Kiery Wright		
Brir Wright		

Appendix: Franklin County, Virginia, 1870 Census

Name	Age	Sex	Color	Occupation	Value of Real Estate	Value of Personal Property	Place of Birth	Married Within Year	Born Within Year	Attended School Within Year	Cannot Read	Cannot Write	Deaf Dumb Blind Insane or or Idiot
204/210 10/05/1870													
John Wright	45	M	M	Farmer			Virginia				1	1	
Susan Wright	50	F	M	Keeping house			Virginia				1	1	
Owen Wright	9	M	M				Virginia						
226/228 10/06/1870													
George Wright	85	M	W	Farmer	1300	100	Virginia						
Porcelia Drury	58	F	W	Keeping house			Virginia				1	1	
Permelia Fuqua	30	F	W	Domestic Servt			Virginia						
Louisa Lynet	28	F	W	Domestic Servt			Virginia						
George Furnis	1	M	W				Virginia						
Callie Linch	10/12	F	W				Virginia			Aug			
227/229 10/06/1870													
Mark Wright	53	M	W	Farmer	1300	1325	Virginia						
James Davis	11	M	W	Farm laborer			Virginia						
229/231 10/06/1870													
Peggy Saunders	75	F	B	Keeping house			Virginia				1	1	
Henry Hollis	55	M	B	Farm laborer			Virginia				1	1	
Catherine Hollis	45	F	B	Keeping house			Virginia				1	1	
Mary Hollis	18	F	B	Without occupation			Virginia				1	1	
James Hollis	15	M	B	Farm laborer			Virginia				1	1	
Jake Hollis	9	M	B				Virginia						
Lydia Hollis	1	F	B				Virginia						
Ada Wright	30	F	B	Farm laborer			Virginia				1	1	
Oatey Wright	15	M	B	Farm laborer			Virginia				1	1	

Appendix: Franklin County, Virginia, 1870 Census

Name [Continued from prior page]	Male Citizen Over 21	Male Citizen Over 21 Without Right to Vote	Identification
204/210 10/05/1870			
John Wright	1		
Susan Wright			
Owen Wright			
226/228 10/06/1870			
George Wright	1		George Finney Wright, son of 1830 William Wright of Franklin County, grandson of 1809 William Wright of Franklin County, and probably great grandson of 1792 John Wright of Fauquier County [apparently listed twice]
Porcelia Drury			
Permelia Fuqua			
Louisa Lynet			
George Furnis			
Callie Linch			
227/229 10/06/1870			
Mark Wright	1		1876 Marquis D[e] L[afayette] Wright of Franklin County, son of George Finney Wright, grandson of 1830 William Wright of Franklin County, and great grandson of 1809 William Wright of Franklin County, and probably great great grandson of 1792 John Wright of Fauquier County
James Davis			
229/231 10/06/1870			
Peggy Saunders			
Henry Hollis	1		
Catherine Hollis			
Mary Hollis			
James Hollis			
Jake Hollis			
Lydia Hollis			
Ada Wright			
Oatey Wright			

Name	Age	Sex	Color	Occupation	Value of Real Estate	Value of Personal Property	Place of Birth	Married Within Year	Born Within Year	Attended School Within Year	Cannot Read	Cannot Write	Deaf Dumb Blind Insane or or Idiot
266/268 10/07/1870													
John Wright	60	M	W	Farmer			Virginia						
Jimmima Wright	58	F	W	Keeping house			Virginia						
George Wright	25	M	W	Farm laborer			Virginia						
William Wright	23	M	W	Farm laborer			Virginia					1	
Joseph Wright	21	M	W	Farm laborer			Virginia					1	
Hastie Whitlow	40	F	W	Domestic Servt			Virginia				1	1	
281/283 10/08/1870													
James Wright	38	M	W	Farmer	100	435	Virginia						
Polly Wright	31	F	W	Keeping house			Virginia						
Henry Howler	56	M	W	Farm Laborer			Virginia						
320/321 10/10/1870													
James Wright	77	M	W	Farmer	600	200	Virginia						
Judith Wright	50	F	W	Keeping house			Virginia						
James Wright	23	M	W	Farm laborer			Virginia						
Thomas Wright	20	M	W	Farm laborer			Virginia						
321/323 10/12/1870													
Millie Wright	42	F	B	Keeping house			Virginia				1	1	
Laticia Wright	16	F	B	Without occupation			Virginia				1	1	
Silas Wright	10	M	B				Virginia				1	1	
Mary Wright	8	F	B				Virginia						
Smith Smith	65	F	B	Domestic Servant			Virginia				1	1	

Appendix: Franklin County, Virginia, 1870 Census

Name [Continued from prior page]	Male Citizen Over 21	Male Citizen Over 21 Without Right to Vote	Identification
266/268 10/07/1870			
John Wright	1		1896 John B. Wright of Franklin County, son of 1823 James Wright of Franklin County, grandson of 1809 William Wright of Franklin County, and probably great grandson of 1792 John Wright of Fauquier County
Jimmima Wright			
George Wright	1		
William Wright	1		
Joseph Wright	1		
Hastie Whitlow			
281/283 10/08/1870			
James Wright	1		1905 James G. Wright of Franklin County, son of 1896 John B. Wright of Franklin County, grandson of 1823 James Wright of Franklin County, and great grandson of 1809 William Wright of Franklin County, and probably great great grandson of 1792 John Wright of Fauquier County
Polly Wright			
Henry Howler	1		
320/321 10/10/1870			
James Wright	1		1877 James Wright of Franklin County, son of 1850 Tommey Wright of Bedford County, grandson of 1803 John Wright of Bedford County, and great grandson of 1763 Thomas Wright of Bedford County
Judith Wright			
James Wright	1		
Thomas Wright			
321/323 10/12/1870			
Millie Wright			
Laticia Wright			
Silas Wright			
Mary Wright			
Smith Smith			

Appendix: Franklin County, Virginia, 1870 Census

Name	Age	Sex	Color	Occupation	Value of Real Estate	Value of Personal Property	Place of Birth	Married Within Year	Born Within Year	Attended School Within Year	Cannot Read	Cannot Write	Deaf Dumb Blind Insane or or Idiot

Snow Creek Thownship

636/477 09/01/1870

Name	Age	Sex	Color	Occupation	Value of Real Estate	Value of Personal Property	Place of Birth	Married Within Year	Born Within Year	Attended School Within Year	Cannot Read	Cannot Write	Deaf Dumb Blind Insane or or Idiot
Langhorn Webb	31	M	W	Farmer	1000	200	Virginia						
Martha Webb	25	F	W	Keeping House			Virginia						
Langhorn Webb	9	M	W				Virginia						
Robert Webb	4	M	W				Virginia						
Henry Webb	1	M	W				Virginia						
Henry Pullen	11	M	B	Domestic Servant			Virginia						
William Wright	13	M	B	Domestic Servant			Virginia				1	1	
Moses Pullen	68	M	B	Farm Laborer			Virginia				1	1	
George Wingfield	58	M	B	Farm Laborer			Virginia				1	1	

Union Hall Township

011/011 08/15/1870

Name	Age	Sex	Color	Occupation	Value of Real Estate	Value of Personal Property	Place of Birth	Married Within Year	Born Within Year	Attended School Within Year	Cannot Read	Cannot Write	Deaf Dumb Blind Insane or or Idiot
John Cundiff	66	M	W	Farmer	800	500	Virginia						
Rhoda Cundiff	56	F	W	Keeps House			Virginia				1	1	
Lydia Cundiff	25	F	W	Weaver			Virginia				1	1	
William Wright	10	M	W				Virginia						

013/013 08/15/1870

Name	Age	Sex	Color	Occupation	Value of Real Estate	Value of Personal Property	Place of Birth	Married Within Year	Born Within Year	Attended School Within Year	Cannot Read	Cannot Write	Deaf Dumb Blind Insane or or Idiot
Frances Wright	35	F	W	Keeps House			Virginia						
John Wright	16	M	W	Farm Laborer			Virginia				1	1	
Victoria Wright	14	F	W	At Home			Virginia				1	1	
Louisa Wright	9	F	W				Virginia						

Appendix: Franklin County, Virginia, 1870 Census

Name [Continued from prior page]	Male Citizen Over 21	Male Citizen Over 21 Without Right to Vote	Identification

Snow Creek Township

636/477 09/01/1870

Name	Male Citizen Over 21	Male Citizen Over 21 Without Right to Vote	Identification
Langhorn Webb	1		
Martha Webb			
Langhorn Webb			
Robert Webb			
Henry Webb			
Henry Pullen			
William Wright			
Moses Pullen	1		
George Wingfield	1		

Union Hall Township

011/011 08/15/1870

Name	Male Citizen Over 21	Male Citizen Over 21 Without Right to Vote	Identification
John Cundiff	1		
Rhoda Cundiff			
Lydia Cundiff			
William Wright			Probably 1920 William J. Wright of Franklin County, son of 1862 Abraham O. Wright of Franklin County, grandson of 1883 Anslem Wright of Franklin County, and great grandson of William Wright

013/013 08/15/1870

Name	Male Citizen Over 21	Male Citizen Over 21 Without Right to Vote	Identification
Frances Wright			Elizabeth Frances (Cundiff) Wright, widow of 1862 Abraham O. Wright of Franklin County, a son of 1883 Anslem Wright of Franklin County and grandson of William Wright
John Wright			
Victoria Wright			
Louisa Wright			

Appendix: Franklin County, Virginia, 1870 Census

Name	Age	Sex	Color	Occupation	Value of Real Estate	Value of Personal Property	Place of Birth	Married Within Year	Born Within Year	Attended School Within Year	Cannot Read	Cannot Write	Deaf Dumb Blind Insane or or Idiot
219/219 08/24/1870													
Longfoot Wright	40	M	B	Farm Laborer			Virginia				1	1	
Emily Wright	31	F	B	Keeps House			Virginia						
Fannie Wright	10	F	B				Virginia						
Nanny Wright	9	F	B				Virginia						
Rosana Wright	7	F	B				Virginia						

Appendix: Franklin County, Virginia, 1870 Census

Name [Continued from prior page]	Male Citizen Over 21	Male Citizen Over 21 Without Right to Vote	Identification
219/219 08/24/1870			
Longfoot Wright	1		Lankford Wright, son of Tandy Graves
Emily Wright			
Fannie Wright			
Nanny Wright			
Rosana Wright			

1880 CENSUS

FRANKLIN COUNTY, VIRGINIA

Appendix: Franklin County, Virginia, 1880 Census

Name	Color	Sex	Age	Monthof Birth	Relationship	Marital Status	Married During Year	Occupation	Months Unem- ployed	Sickness Blind Deaf & Dumb Idiotic Disabled
Blackwater District										
8th day of June, 1880										
Dwelling #50/Family #50										
Latitia Wright	B	F	25					Keeping House		
James W Wright	B	M	9		Son					
Tazewell H Wright	B	M	6		Son					
John L Wright	B	M	4		Son					
10th day of June 1880										
Dwelling #85/Family #85										
Julious Stepto	B	M	50			M		Farmer		
Phillis Stepto	B	F	40		wife	M		Keeping House		
Frances Stepto	B	F	17		daughter	M		At Home		
Robert Stepto	B	M	14		son	S		Farm Laborer		
William Stepto	B	M	13		son	S		Farm Laborer		
____sy Calloway	B	M	23		Stepson	S		Farm Laborer		
Jack Wright	B	M	25		son law	M		Farm Laborer		
George H Wright	B	M	3		Gran son	S		At Home		
Sallie Wright	B	F	2		" daughter	S		At Home		
Dwelling #95/Family #95										
Samuel Wright	B	M	29			M		Farm Laborer		
Ellen Wright	B	F	24		wife	M		Keeping House		
Thomas Wright	B	M	7		son	S		at home		
Roberta Wright	B	F	4		Daughter	S		at home		
Reubin H Wright	B	M	1		Son	S				
Millie Wright	B	F	54		Mother	W		at home		

Appendix: Franklin County, Virginia, 1880 Census

Name continued from previous page]	Attended School Within Year	Cannot Read	Cannot Write	Born	Father Born	Mother Born	Identification
Blackwater District							
8th day of June, 1880							
Dwelling #50/Family #50							
Latitia Wright			1	Virginia	Va	Va	
James W Wright				Virginia	Va	Va	
Tazewell H Wright				Virginia	Va	Va	
John L Wright				Virginia	Va	Va	
10th day of June 1880							
Dwelling #85/Family #85							
Julious Stepto		1	1	Virginia	Va	Va	
Phillis Stepto		1	1	Virginia	Va	Va	
Frances Stepto		1	1	Virginia	Va	Va	
Robert Stepto		1	1	Virginia	Va	Va	
William Stepto		1	1	Virginia	Va	Va	
____sy Calloway		1	1	Virginia	Va	Va	
Jack Wright		1	1	Virginia	Va	Va	
George H Wright				Virginia	Va	Va	
Sallie Wright				Virginia	Va	Va	
Dwelling #95/Family #95							
Samuel Wright		1	1	Virginia	Va	Va	Samuel Wright, son of James Wright
Ellen Wright		1	1	Virginia	Va	Va	
Thomas Wright	1			Virginia	Va	Va	
Roberta Wright				Virginia	Va	Va	
Reubin H Wright				Virginia	Va	Va	
Millie Wright		1	1	Virginia	Va	Va	

Name	Color	Sex	Age	Month of Birth	Relationship	Marital Status	Married During Year	Occupation	Months Unem- ployed	Sickness Blind Deaf & Dumb Idiotic Disabled

12th day of June 1880

Dwelling #129/Family #129

Name	Color	Sex	Age	Month of Birth	Relationship	Marital Status	Married During Year	Occupation	Months Unemployed	Sickness/Blind/Deaf & Dumb/Idiotic/Disabled
David Wright	W	M	26			M		Farm Laborer		
Mary E Wright	W	F	28		wife	M		Keeping House		
John C. Wright	W	M	5		son	S		At Home		
James G Wright	W	M	3		Son	S		At Home		
George T Wright	W	M	2		son	S		At Home		
Bettie A. Wright	W	F	8/12		Daughter	S		At Home		

15th day of June 1880

Dwelling #173/Family #173

Name	Color	Sex	Age	Month of Birth	Relationship	Marital Status	Married During Year	Occupation	Months Unemployed	Sickness/Blind/Deaf & Dumb/Idiotic/Disabled
Crockett Wright	W	M	56			M		Farmer		
Ruthy E. Wright	W	F	55		Wife	M				Blind
William B. Wright	W	M	21		son	M		Farm Hand		
Arkansas Wright	W	F	21		Daug law	M		Keeping House		
George A Wright	W	M	19		son	M		Farm Hand		
Elizabeth A. Wright	W	F	24		Daug law	M		At Home		
Joel T. Wright	W	M	16		son	S		Farm Hand		
Surrena T. Wright	W	F	24		daughter	S		At Home		
Rufus Wright	W	M	1		Granson	S		At Home		
Nancy E. Wright	W	F	6/12		Grn Daughter	S		At Home		

Name continued from previous page]	Attended School Within Year	Cannot Read	Cannot Write	Born	Father Born	Mother Born	Identification
12th day of June 1880							
Dwelling #129/Family #129							
David Wright	1	1		Virginia	Va	Va	David S. Wright, son of 1901 Crockett Anderson Wright of
Mary E Wright				Virginia	Va	Va	Franklin County and grandson of Smith Wright (Montgomery
John C. Wright				Virginia	Va	Va	County)
James G Wright				Virginia	Va	Va	
George T Wright				Virginia	Va	Va	
Bettie A. Wright				Virginia	Va	Va	
15th day of June 1880							
Dwelling #173/Family #173							
Crockett Wright	1	1		Virginia	Va	Va	1901 Crockett Anderson Wright of Franklin County, son of
Ruthy E. Wright	1	1		Virginia	Va	Va	Smith Wright (Montgomery County)
William B. Wright1	1	1		Virginia	Va	Va	
Arkansas Wrigh1	1	1		Virginia	Va	Va	
George A Wright				Virginia	Va	Va	
Elizabeth A. Wright			1	Virginia	Va	Va	
Joel T. Wright	1	1		Virginia	Va	Va	
Surrena T. Wright	1	1		Virginia	Va	Va	
Rufus Wright				Virginia	Va	Va	
Nancy E. Wright				Virginia	Va	Va	

Appendix: Franklin County, Virginia, 1880 Census

Name	Color	Sex	Age	Month of Birth	Relationship	Marital Status	Married During Year	Occupation	Months Unemployed	Sickness Blind Deaf & Dumb Idiotic Disabled
Dwelling #299/Family #300										
Isaac Wright	W	M	32			M		Farmer		
Oney Wright	W	F	31		wife	M		Keeping House		
Jacob A. Wright	W	M	9		son	S		At Home		
Henry C. Wright	W	M	8		son	S		At Home		
Lucy E. Wright	W	F	7		daughter	S		At Home		
Rejina Wright	W	F	4		daughter	S		At Home		
Isaac M. Wright	W	M	3		son	S		At Home		
Mary L. Wright	W	F	1		daughter	S		At Home		
Lucy Sigman	W	F	19		servant	S		Servant		

Ronbrook District page 6
4th & 5th days of June, 1880

Name	Color	Sex	Age	Month of Birth	Relationship	Marital Status	Married During Year	Occupation	Months Unemployed	Sickness Blind Deaf & Dumb Idiotic Disabled
Dwelling #51/ Family #51										
Henry S. Wright	W	M	30			M		Farmer		
Sallie E. Wright	W	F	29		Wife	M		Keeping House		
Joseph L. Wright	W	M	8		Son	S				
Sarah L. Wright	W	F	7		Daughter	S				
Robert A. Wright	W	M	5		Son	S				
Rhoda C. Wright	W	F	3		Daughter	S				

Name continued from previous page]	Attended School Within Year	Cannot Read	Cannot Write	Born	Father Born	Mother Born	Identification
Dwelling #299/Family #300							
Isaac Wright			1	Virginia	Va	Va	1918 Isaac M. Wright of Franklin County, son of 1901
Oney Wright			1	Virginia	Va	Va	Crockett Anderson Wright of Franklin County and grandson of
Jacob A. Wright			1	Virginia	Va	Va	Smith Wright (Montgomery County)
Henry C. Wright				Virginia	Va	Va	
Lucy E. Wright				Virginia	Va	Va	
Rejina Wright				Virginia	Va	Va	
Isaac M. Wright				Virginia	Va	Va	
Mary L. Wright				Virginia	Va	Va	
Lucy Sigman		1	1	Virginia	Va	Va	

Ronbrook District
4th & 5th days of June, 1880

Dwelling #51/ Family #51

Name				Born	Father Born	Mother Born	Identification
Henry S. Wright				Virginia	Va	Va	Henry Smith Wright, son of 1890 Robert Penn Wright of
Sallie E. Wright				Virginia	Va	Va	Franklin County, grandson of 1849 Thomas Wright of Franklin
Joseph L. Wright				Virginia	Va	Va	County, great grandson of 1815 Joseph Wright of Bedford
Sarah L. Wright				Virginia	Va	Va	County and great grandson of 1803 John Wright of Bedford
Robert A. Wright				Virginia	Va	Va	County, and great great grandson of 1763 Thomas Wright of
Rhoda C. Wright				Virginia	Va	Va	Bedford County

Appendix: Franklin County, Virginia, 1880 Census

Name	Color	Sex	Age	Monthof Birth	Relationship	Marital Status	Married During Year	Occupation	Months Unem- ployed	Sickness Blind Deaf & Dumb Idiotic Disabled

8th & 9th days of June, 1880

Dwelling #86/Family #86

Name	Color	Sex	Age	Monthof Birth	Relationship	Marital Status	Married During Year	Occupation	Months Unem- ployed	Disabled
Thos F Taylor Jr	W	M	60			W		Farmer		
James T Taylor	W	M	27		Son	S		Laborer	2	
Thos F Taylor Jr	W	M	24		Son	S		Physician		
Theo S Taylor	W	M	19		Son	S		Laborer	3	
Mary J. Taylor	W	F	17		Daughter	S		At Home		
Moss Taylor	W	M	10		Son	S		Laborer	4	
Susan T Wright	W	F	39		Sister in Law	S		Keeping House		
Hank Brooks	B	M	24		Boarder	S		Laborer	12	
Orange Taylor	B	M	30		Boarder	M		Laborer	2	
Nancy Riss	B	F	40		Servant	S		Servant		
Rhoda Riss	B	F	10		Servant	S		Servant		
James Turnin	M	M	10		Laborer	S		Laborer	__(?)	

19th & 21st days of June, 1880

Dwelling #267/Family #267

Name	Color	Sex	Age	Monthof Birth	Relationship	Marital Status	Married During Year	Occupation	Months Unem- ployed	Disabled
Asa Wright	W	M	64			M		Farmer		
Polly Wright	W	F	64		Wife	M		Keeping House		
Thomas Brooks	B	M	10		Boarder	S		Laborer		
Peter Dillin	B	M	14		Boarder	S		Laborer		

Appendix: Franklin County, Virginia, 1880 Census

Name continued from previous page]	Attended School Within Year	Cannot Read	Cannot Write	Born	Father Born	Mother Born	Identification

8th & 9th days of June, 1880

Dwelling #86/Family #86

Thos F Taylor Jr				Virginia	Va	Va	Susan T. Wright, daughter of 1845 William Wright of Franklin
James T Taylor				Virginia	Va	Va	County, granddaughter of 1830 William Wright of Franklin
Thos F Taylor Jr				Virginia	Va	Va	County, great granddaughter of 1809 William Wright of Franklin
Theo S Taylor				Virginia	Va	Va	County, and probably great great granddaughter of 1792
Mary J. Taylor				Virginia	Va	Va	John Wright of Fauquier County
Moss Taylor				Virginia	Va	Va	
Susan T Wright				Virginia	Va	Va	
Hank Brooks		1	1	Virginia	Va	Va	
Orange Taylor		1	1	Virginia	Va	Va	
Nancy Riss		1	1	Virginia	Va	Va	
Rhoda Riss		1	1	Virginia	Va	Va	
James Turnin		1	1	Virginia	Va	Va	

19th & 21st days of June, 1880

Dwelling #267/Family #267

Asa Wright				Virginia	Va	Va	1901 Asa Wright of Franklin County, son of 1839 John A.
Polly Wright				Virginia	Va	Va	Wright of Franklin County, grandson of 1830 William Wright of
Thomas Brooks		1	1	Virginia	Va	Va	Franklin County, great grandson of 1809 William Wright of
Peter Dillin			1	Virginia	Va	Va	Franklin County, and probably great great grandson of 1792
							John Wright of Fauquier County

Appendix: Franklin County, Virginia, 1880 Census

Name	Color	Sex	Age	Month of Birth	Relationship	Marital Status	Married During Year	Occupation	Months Unem- ployed	Sickness Blind Deaf & Dumb Idiotic Disabled
Dwelling #271/ Family #271										
James K. Wright	W	M	36			M		Laborer	3	
Polly A. Wright	W	F	26		Wife	M		Keeping House		
Cora L. Wright	W	F	9		Daughter	S				
Bettie C. Wright	W	F	6		Daughter	S				
James A. Wright	W	M	4		Son	S				
Jennie F. Wright	W	F	1		Daughter	S				
Dwelling #282/Family #272										
Joshua Wright Sr.	B	M	57			M		Laborer	3	
Julia Wright	Mu	F	54		Wife	M		Keeping House		
Mariah Burwell	Mu	F	11		Niece	S		At Home		
Dandrig Burwell	Mu	M	2		Nephew	S				
Dwelling #284/Family #284										
Albert Kingery	W	M	64			M		Farmer		
Usley Kingery	W	F	62		Wife	M		Keeping House		
Cathrine Kingery	W	F	23		Daughter	S		At Home		
Thomas Kingery	W	M	21		Son	S		Laborer	1	
Ann E Kingery	W	F	17		Daughter	S		At Home		
Susan Wright	W	F	35		Daughter	W		at Home		
Usley Wright	W	F	10		Grand Daug	S		at Home		

Name continued from previous page]	Attended School Within Year	Cannot Read	Cannot Write	Born	Father Born	Mother Born	Identification
Dwelling #271/ Family #271							
James K. Wright		1	1	Virginia	Va	Va	James K. Wright, son of 1883 Anslem Wright of Franklin
Polly A. Wright				Virginia	Va	Va	County and grandson of William Wright
Cora L. Wright				Virginia	Va	Va	
Bettie C. Wright				Virginia	Va	Va	
James A. Wright				Virginia	Va	Va	
Jennie F. Wright				Virginia	Va	Va	
Dwelling #282/Family #272							
Joshua Wright Sr.		1	1	Virginia	Va	Va	
Julia Wright		1	1	Virginia	Va	Va	
Mariah Burwell		1	1	Virginia	Va	Va	
Dandrig Burwell				Virginia	Va	Va	
Dwelling #284/Family #284							
Albert Kingery		1	1	Virginia	Va	Va	Susan Wright, daughter of Ursley (Wright) Kingery,
Usley Kingery		1	1	Virginia	Va	Va	granddaughter of Jane (Wright) Arthur, great granddaughter of
Cathrine Kingery			1	Virginia	Va	Va	1823 James Wright of Franklin County, great great
Thomas Kingery			1	Virginia	Va	Va	granddaughter of 1809 William Wright of Franklin County, and
Ann E Kingery				Virginia	Va	Va	probably great great great granddaughter of 1792 John Wright
Susan Wright				Virginia	Va	Va	of Fauquier County
Usley Wright		1	1	Virginia	Va	Va	

Name	Color	Sex	Age	Monthof Birth	Relationship	Marital Status	Married During Year	Occupation	Months Unem- ployed	Sickness Blind Deaf & Dumb Idiotic Disabled

22nd day of June, 1880

Dwelling #304/Family #304

Name	Color	Sex	Age	Monthof Birth	Relationship	Marital Status	Married During Year	Occupation	Months Unem- ployed	Sickness Blind Deaf & Dumb Idiotic Disabled
Wesley Wright	B	M	35			M		Farmer		
Cathrine Wright	B	F	30		Wife	M		Keeping House		
James Wright	B	M	13		Son	S		Laborer	1	
John Wright	B	M	11		Son	S		Laborer	1	
Cathrine Wright	B	F	10		Daughter	S		At Home		
Green Wright	B	M	8		Son	S				
Julia Wright	B	F	5		Daughter	S				
Lewis Wright	B	M	4		Son	S				
William Wright	B	M	3		Son	S				
Thomas Wright	B	M	1		Son	S				

22nd & 23rd days of June, 1880

Dwelling #312/Family #312

Name	Color	Sex	Age	Monthof Birth	Relationship	Marital Status	Married During Year	Occupation	Months Unem- ployed	Sickness Blind Deaf & Dumb Idiotic Disabled
Plesant Wright	B	M	57			M		Black Smith		
Agness Wright	Mu	F	50		Wife	M		Keeping House		
Manassa Wright	Mu	F	20		Daughter	S		At Home		
Mariah Wright	Mu	F	18		Daughter	S		At Home		
Robt Wright	Mu	M	14		Son	S		Laborer		
Charles Wright	Mu	M	10		Son	S		Laborer		
Mariah Claiborn	B	F	80		Mother in Law	W		At Home		

Name continued from previous page]	Attended School Within Year	Cannot Read	Cannot Write	Born	Father Born	Mother Born	Identification
22nd day of June, 1880							
Dwelling #304/Family #304							
Wesley Wright	1		1	Virginia	Va	Va	John Wesley Wright, son of Joshua Wright
Cathrine Wright	1		1	Virginia	Va	Va	
James Wright	1		1	Virginia	Va	Va	
John Wright	1		1	Virginia	Va	Va	
Cathrine Wright	1		1	Virginia	Va	Va	
Green Wright				Virginia	Va	Va	
Julia Wright				Virginia	Va	Va	
Lewis Wright				Virginia	Va	Va	
William Wright				Virginia	Va	Va	
Thomas Wright				Virginia	Va	Va	
22nd & 23rd days of June, 1880							
Dwelling #312/Family #312							
Plesant Wright	1		1	Virginia	Va	Va	1898 Pleasant Wright of Franklin County
Agness Wright	1		1	Virginia	Va	Va	
Manassa Wright	1		1	Virginia	Va	Va	
Mariah Wright	1		1	Virginia	Va	Va	
Robt Wright			1	Virginia	Va	Va	
Charles Wright	1		1	Virginia	Va	Va	
Mariah Claiborn	1		1	Virginia	Va	Va	

Appendix: Franklin County, Virginia, 1880 Census

Name	Color	Sex	Age	Month of Birth	Relationship	Marital Status	Married During Year	Occupation	Months Unem- ployed	Sickness Blind Deaf & Dumb Idiotic Disabled

<u>23rd & 24th days of June, 1880</u>

Dwelling #325/Family #325

Name	Color	Sex	Age	Month of Birth	Relationship	Marital Status	Married During Year	Occupation	Months Unem- ployed	Disabled
Robert P. Wright	W	M	58			M		Farmer		
Rhoda Wright	W	F	62		Wife	M		Keeping House		
Milton M Wright	W	M	27		Son	S		Laborer	1	
Cisaroe A. Wright	W	M	24		Son	S		Laborer	1	
Nancy L Wright	W	F	18		Daughter	S		At Home		

<u>24th day of June, 1880</u>

Dwelling #335/Family #335

Name	Color	Sex	Age	Month of Birth	Relationship	Marital Status	Married During Year	Occupation	Months Unem- ployed	Disabled
Stephen Kasey	B	M	25			M		Farmer		
Martha Kasey	B	F	34		Wife	M		Keeping House		
Catherine Kasey	B	F	18		Sister	S		At Home		
William C Wright	B	M	8		Bound	S				

Dwelling #337/Family #337

Name	Color	Sex	Age	Month of Birth	Relationship	Marital Status	Married During Year	Occupation	Months Unem- ployed	Disabled
Leaoky Wright	B	F	25			S		Keeping House		
Louisa Wright	B	F	5		Daughter	S				
Frances Wright	B	F	2		Daughter	S				

Appendix: Franklin County, Virginia, 1880 Census

Name continued from previous page]	Attended School Within Year	Cannot Read	Cannot Write	Born	Father Born	Mother Born	Identification

23rd & 24th days of June, 1880

Dwelling #325/Family #325

Robert P. Wright				Virginia	Va	Va	1890 Robert Penn Wright of Franklin County, son of 1849
Rhoda Wright				Virginia	Va	Va	Thomas Wright of Franklin County, grandson of 1815 Joseph
Milton M Wright				Virginia	Va	Va	Wright of Bedford County and grandson of 1803 John Wright of
Cisaroe A. Wright				Virginia	Va	Va	Bedford County, and great grandson of 1763 Thomas Wright of
Nancy L Wright				Virginia	Va	Va	Bedford County

24th day of June, 1880

Dwelling #335/Family #335

Stephen Kasey		1	1	Virginia	Va	Va	
Martha Kasey		1	1	Virginia	Va	Va	
Catherine Kasey		1	1	Virginia	Va	Va	
William C Wright				Virginia	Va	Va	

Dwelling #337/Family #337

Leaoky Wright		1	1	Virginia	Va	Va	
Louisa Wright				Virginia	Va	Va	
Frances Wright				Virginia	Va	Va	

Name	Color	Sex	Age	Month of Birth	Relationship	Marital Status	Married During Year	Occupation	Months Unemployed	Sickness Blind Deaf & Dumb Idiotic Disabled
Dwelling #383/Family #383										
William T. Wright	W	M	39			M		Farmer		
Octavia M. Wright	W	F	38		Wife	M		Keeping House		
John H R. Wright	W	M	14		Son	S		Laborer		
Ida M. Wright	W	F	12		Daughter	S		At Home		
William P. Wright	W	M	9		Son	S				
James C. Wright	W	M	5		Son	S				
Rosco Wright	W	M	3		Son	S				
no name Wright	W		5/12		Son	S		dec. son		
John Hatcher	B	M	19		Boarder	S		Laborer	1	

Brown Hill District
19 & 22st days of June, 1880

Name	Color	Sex	Age	Month of Birth	Relationship	Marital Status	Married During Year	Occupation	Months Unemployed	Sickness Blind Deaf & Dumb Idiotic Disabled
Dwelling #336/Family #336										
John H. Right	W	M	25			M		Farmer		
Nancy E. Right	W	F	22		Wife	M		Keeping House		
Amanda Right	W	F	4		Daughter	S				
Lillie Right	W	F	2		Daughter	S				
William Right	W	M	3/12	Mar	Son	S				

Name continued from previous page]	Attended School Within Year	Cannot Read	Cannot Write	Born	Father Born	Mother Born	Identification
Dwelling #383/Family #383							
William T. Wright				Virginia	Va	Va	1928 William Thomas Wright, son of 1890 Robert Penn Wright
Octavia M. Wright				Virginia	Va	Va	of Franklin County, grandson of 1849 Thomas Wright of
John H R. Wright				Virginia	Va	Va	Franklin County, great grandson of 1815 Joseph Wright of
Ida M. Wright				Virginia	Va	Va	Bedford County and great grandson of 1803 John Wright of
William P. Wright				Virginia	Va	Va	Bedford County, and great great grandson of 1763 Thomas
James C. Wright				Virginia	Va	Va	Wright of Bedford County
Rosco Wright				Virginia	Va	Va	
no name Wright				Virginia	Va	Va	
John Hatcher		1	1	Virginia	Va	Va	
Brown Hill District							
19 & 22st days of June, 1880							
Dwelling #336/Family #336							
John H. Right		1	1	Virginia	Va	Va	John Henry Wright, son of 1901 Crockett Anderson Wright of
Nancy E. Right				Virginia	Va	Va	Franklin County and grandson of Smith Wright (Montgomery
Amanda Right				Virginia	Va	Va	County)
Lillie Right				Virginia	Va	Va	
William Right				Virginia	Va	Va	

Appendix: Franklin County, Virginia, 1880 Census

Name	Color	Sex	Age	Monthof Birth	Relationship	Marital Status	Married During Year	Occupation	Months Unem- ployed	Sickness Blind Deaf & Dumb Idiotic Disabled

Gills Creek District
1st day of June, 1880

Dwelling #2/Family #2

Name	Color	Sex	Age	Monthof Birth	Relationship	Marital Status	Married During Year	Occupation	Months Unem- ployed	Sickness Blind Deaf & Dumb Idiotic Disabled
Harrison J Hancock	W	M	41			M		Farmer		
Fannie S Hancock	W	F	43		Wife	M		Keeping House		
Ada N Hancock	W	F	13		Daughter	S		At School		
Harry H Hancock	W	M	8		Son	S		At School		
Mattie L. Hancock	W	F	3		Daughter	S				
Martha Hatcher	W	F	75		Mother in law	W		At home	12	
J M Merriman	W	M	30		Boarder	S		Merchant		
Poka Hancock	B	F	15		Servant	S		Domestic Work		
Leticia Holland	B	F	25		Servant	M		Cooking		
Ada Saunders	B	F	7		Servant	M				
Wm Ferquson	B	M	2		Servant	S				
Otho Wright	B	M	12		Servant	S		Works on Farm		

3d & 4th day of June, 1880

Dwelling #21/Family #21

Name	Color	Sex	Age	Monthof Birth	Relationship	Marital Status	Married During Year	Occupation	Months Unem- ployed	Sickness Blind Deaf & Dumb Idiotic Disabled
Joseph K. Wright	W	M	70			M		Farmer		
Sarah R. Wright	W	F	68		Wife	M		Keeping House		
Thomas Harman	W	M	44		Servant	S		Farm Hand		
Henrietta Turner	B	F	18		Servant	D		Domestic Work		Idiotic
Robt L Dent	B	M	6		Servant	S				

Appendix: Franklin County, Virginia, 1880 Census

Name continued from previous page]	Attended School Within Year	Cannot Read	Cannot Write	Born	Father Born	Mother Born	Identification
Gills Creek District							
1st day of June, 1880							
Dwelling #2/Family #2							
Harrison J Hancock				Va	Va	Va	
Fannie S Hancock				Va	Va	Va	
Ada N Hancock	1			Va	Va	Va	
Harry H Hancock	1			Va	Va	Va	
Mattie L. Hancock				Va	Va	Va	
Martha Hatcher				Va	Va	Va	
J M Merriman				Va	Va	Va	
Poka Hancock		1	1	Va	Va	Va	
Leticia Holland		1	1	Va	Va	Va	
Ada Saunders				Va	Va	Va	
Wm Ferguson				Va	Va	Va	
Otho Wright		1	1	Va	Va	Va	
3d & 4th day of June, 1880							
Dwelling #21/Family #21							
Joseph K. Wright				Va	Va	Va	Joseph Kemp Wright, son of 1855 Wright Wright of Franklin
Sarah R. Wright			1	Va	Va	Va	County, grandson of 1815 Joseph Wright of Bedford County,
Thomas Harman		1	1	Va	Va	Va	and great grandson of 1763 Thomas Wright of Bedford County
Henrietta Turner		1	1	Va	Va	Va	
Robt L Dent				Va	Va	Va	

Appendix: Franklin County, Virginia, 1880 Census

Name	Color	Sex	Age	Month of Birth	Relationship	Marital Status	Married During Year	Occupation	Months Unem- ployed	Sickness Blind Deaf & Dumb Idiotic Disabled
Dwelling #34/ Family #34										
James Thomerson	W	M	74			M		Farmer		
Minerva R Thomerson	W	F	64			M		Keeping house		
Thomas Parker Thomerson	W	M	25			S		Farm hand		
Tish Brown	B	F	17		Servant	S		Farm hand		
Green Wright	B	M	9		Servant	S				
Dwelling #69/Family #69										
F.J.T. Wright	W	M	58			S		Farmer		
Henry S. Wright	W	M	44		Brother	S		Farmer		
Mary A. Wright	W	F	43		Sister	S		Keeping house		
Judith Wright	B	F	80		Servant	S		Domestic Work		
Dwelling #108/Family #110										
Laurence M. Wright	W	M	32			M		Farmer		
Nancy J. Wright	W	F	33		Wife	M		Keeping house		
Dellah R. Wright	W	F	7		Daughter	S		At home		
Susanna B. Wright	W	F	2		Daughter	S				
John R Amrose	W	M	12		Servant	S		Farm Hand		
Louisa Burwell	W	F	17		Servant	S		Domestic Work		

Appendix: Franklin County, Virginia, 1880 Census

Name continued from previous page]	Attended School Within Year	Cannot Read	Cannot Write	Born	Father Born	Mother Born	Identification
Dwelling #34/ Family #34							
James Thomerson				Va	Va	Va	
Minerva R Thomerson				Va	Va	Va	
Thomas Parker Thomerson				Va	Va	Va	
Tish Brown				Va	Va	Va	
Green Wright				Va	Va	Va	
Dwelling #69/Family #69							
F.J.T. Wright				Va	Va	Va	1901 Fleming J. T. Wright of Franklin County, son of 1855
Henry S. Wright				Va	Va	Va	Wright Wright of Franklin County, grandson of 1815 Joseph
Mary A. Wright				Va	Va	Va	Wright of Bedford County, and great grandson of 1763 Thomas
Judith Wright		1	1	Va	Va	Va	Wright of Bedford County
Dwelling #108/Family #110							
Laurence M. Wright				Va	Va	Va	1933 Laurence Monroe Wright of Franklin County, son of 1890
Nancy J. Wright				Va	Va	Va	Robert Penn Wright of Franklin County, grandson of 1849
Dellah R. Wright	1			Va	Va	Va	Thomas Wright of Franklin County, great grandson of 1815
Susanna B. Wright				Va	Va	Va	Joseph Wright of Bedford County and great grandson of 1803
John R Amrose	1		1	Va	Va	Va	John Wright of Bedford County, and great great grandson of
Louisa Burwell		1	1	Va	Va	Va	1763 Thomas Wright of Bedford County

Name	Color	Sex	Age	Month of Birth	Relationship	Marital Status	Married During Year	Occupation	Months Unemployed	Sickness Blind Deaf & Dumb Idiotic Disabled
104 Enumeration District										
Eighth day of June, 1880										
Dwelling #91/Family #91										
Anslem Wright	W	M	75			M		Farmer		
Margaret Wright	W	F	38		Wife	M		Keeping house		
Poky Wright	W	F	12		Stepdaughter	S		Keeping house		
Wilmuth A. J. Wright	W	F	12		Granddaughter	S		Keeping house		
Tenth Eleventh days of June 1880										
Dwelling #135/Family #135										
William R. Wright	W	M	53			M		Blacksmith		
Eliza Ann Wright	W	F	46		Wife	M		Keeping house		
Samuel L.T. Wright	W	M	22		Son	S		Blacksmith		
Louretta C. Wright	W	F	13		Daughter	S		Keeping house		
Amanda E. Wright	W	F	9		Daughter	S				
Eliza W. Wright	W	F	7		Daughter	S				
Dwelling #372/Family #372										
Andrew J. Wright	W	M	42			M		Farmer		
Sarah Jane Wright	W	F	29		Wife	M		Keeping house		
Oliver J. Wright	W	M	12		Son	S		Farm hand		

Name continued from previous page]	Attended School Within Year	Cannot Read	Cannot Write	Born	Father Born	Mother Born	Identification
104 Enumeration District Eighth day of June, 1880							
Dwelling #91/Family #91							
Anslem Wright		1	1	Virginia	Virginia	Virginia	1883 Anslem Wright of Franklin County, son of William Wright
Margaret Wright				Virginia	Virginia	Virginia	
Poky Wright	1			Virginia	Virginia	Virginia	
Wilmuth A. J. Wright	1		1	Virginia	Virginia	Virginia	
Tenth Eleventh days of June 1880							
Dwelling #135/Family #135							
William R. Wright				Virginia	Virginia	Virginia	1884 William R. Wright of Franklin County, son of 1883 Anslem
Eliza Ann Wright		1	1	Virginia	Virginia	Virginia	Wright of Franklin County and grandson of William Wright
Samuel L.T. Wright		1	1	Virginia	Virginia	Virginia	
Louretta C. Wright	1			Virginia	Virginia	Virginia	
Amanda E. Wright				Virginia	Virginia	Virginia	
Eliza W. Wright				Virginia	Virginia	Virginia	
Dwelling #372/Family #372							
Andrew J. Wright		1	1	Virginia	Virginia	Virginia	Andrew J. Wright of Bedford County, son of 1883 Anslem
Sarah Jane Wright				Virginia	Virginia	Virginia	Wright of Franklin County and grandson of William Wright
Oliver J. Wright				Virginia	Virginia	Virginia	

Name	Color	Sex	Age	Month of Birth	Relationship	Marital Status	Married During Year	Occupation	Months Unemployed	Sickness Blind Deaf & Dumb Idiotic Disabled

Long Branch District
1st day of June 1880

Dwelling #240/Family #240

Name	Color	Sex	Age	Month of Birth	Relationship	Marital Status	Married During Year	Occupation	Months Unemployed	Sickness Blind Deaf & Dumb Idiotic Disabled
John Wright	W		27			S		Laborer		
Sarah Wright	W		60		Mother	M		Keeping house		
Martha Wright	W		23		Sister	S		At home		

Maggodee Creek District
4th day of June, 1880

Dwelling #61/Family #61

Name	Color	Sex	Age	Month of Birth	Relationship	Marital Status	Married During Year	Occupation	Months Unemployed	Sickness Blind Deaf & Dumb Idiotic Disabled
G. G. Wright	W	M	34			M		Farmer		
A. Calla Wright	W	F	26		wife	M		Keeping house		
Cordelia Wright	W	F	8		daughter	S		At home		
Alice Wright	W	F	7		daughter	S		At home		
J. Emma Wright	W	F	3		daughter	S		At home		
John B. Wright	W	M	71		Father	W		Farmer		

Dwelling #62/Family #62

Name	Color	Sex	Age	Month of Birth	Relationship	Marital Status	Married During Year	Occupation	Months Unemployed	Sickness Blind Deaf & Dumb Idiotic Disabled
Abram Wright	W	M	38			M		Farmer		
Nancy Wright	W	F	28		wife	M		Keeps house		
James Wright	W	M	12		son	S		At home		
John Wright	W	M	8		son	S		At home		
Charley Wright	W	M	6		son	S		At home		
Jefferson Wright	W	M	2		son	S		At home		

Name continued from previous page]	Attended School Within Year	Cannot Read	Cannot Write	Born	Father Born	Mother Born	Identification
Long Branch District **1st day of June 1880**							
Dwelling #240/Family #240							
John Wright				Virginia	Va	Va	
Sarah Wright		1	1	Virginia	Va	Va	
Martha Wright		1	1	Virginia	Va	Va	
Maggodee Creek District **4th day of June, 1880**							
Dwelling #61/Family #61							
G. G. Wright			1	Virginia	Va	Va	George Greenberry Wright, son of 1896 John B. Wright of
A. Calla Wright				Virginia	Va	Va	Franklin County, grandson of 1823 James Wright of Franklin
Cordelia Wright	1			Virginia	Va	Va	County, great grandson of 1809 William Wright Wright of
Alice Wright	1			Virginia	Va	Va	Franklin County, and probably great great grandson of 1792
J. Emma Wright				Virginia	Va	Va	John Wright of Fauquier County
John B. Wright		1	1	Virginia	Va	Va	
Dwelling #62/Family #62							
Abram Wright		1	1	Virginia	Va	Va	Abraham H. Wright, son of 1896 John B. Wright of Franklin
Nancy Wright			1	Virginia	Va	Va	County, grandson of 1823 James Wright of Franklin County,
James Wright	1		1	Virginia	Va	Va	great grandson of 1809 William Wright Wright of Franklin
John Wright	1			Virginia	Va	Va	County, and probably great great grandson of 1792 John
Charley Wright				Virginia	Va	Va	Wright of Fauquier County
Jefferson Wright				Virginia	Va	Va	

Appendix: Franklin County, Virginia, 1880 Census

Name	Color	Sex	Age	Monthof Birth	Relationship	Marital Status	Married During Year	Occupation	Months Unem- ployed	Sickness Blind Deaf & Dumb Idiotic Disabled
Dwelling #63/ Family #63										
Wm J. Wright	W	M	36			M		Farm laborer		
Mary Wright	W	F	35		wife	M		Keeps house		
Charlotte Wright	W	F	15		daughter	S		At home		
Rocky Mount District										
11 & 12 days of June, 1880										
Dwelling #262/Family #262										
Elaine Wright	B	F	30			S		Keeping Houce		
Minnie Wright	B	F	4		Daughter	S				
Ellen Wright	B	F	2		Daughter	S				
James Wright	B	M	3/12	Feb	son	S				
Georgia Fry	B	F	3		Boarder	S				
Babe Fry	B	F	5/12	Dec	Boarder	S				
Union Hall District										
14 day of June, 1880										
Dwelling #80/ Family #81										
Thomas Dudley Sr	W	M	75			M		Farmer		
Liddy M. Dudley	W	F	35		Wife	M		Keeping House		
Lula V. Dudley	W	F	8		daughter	S		at school		
Wilson A. J. Wright	W	M	21		Broth law	S		Farm labourer		

Name continued from previous page]	Attended School Within Year	Cannot Read	Cannot Write	Born	Father Born	Mother Born	Identification
Dwelling #63/ Family #63							
Wm J. Wright			1	Virginia	Va	Va	William J. Wright, son of 1896 John B. Wright of Franklin County, grandson of 1823 James Wright of Franklin County, great grandson of 1809 William Wright of Franklin County, and probably great great grandson of 1792 John Wright of Fauquier County
Mary Wright		1	1	Virginia	Va	Va	
Charlotte Wright		1	1	Virginia	Va	Va	
Rocky Mount District **11 & 12 days of June, 1880**							
Dwelling #262/Family #262							
Elaine Wright		1	1	Virginia	Va	Va	
Minnie Wright				Virginia	Va	Va	
Ellen Wright				Virginia	Va	Va	
James Wright				Virginia	Va	Va	
Georgia Fry				Virginia	Va	Va	
Babe Fry				Virginia	Va	Va	
Union Hall District **17 day of June, 1880**							
Dwelling #80/ Family #81							
Thomas Dudley Sr				Va	Va	Va	1920 Wilson J. Wright of Franklin County, son of 1862 Abraham O. Wright of Franklin County, grandson of 1883 Anslem Wright of Franklin County, and great grandson of William Wright
Liddy M. Dudley				Va	Va	Va	
Lula V. Dudley	1			Va	Va	Va	
Wilson A. J. Wright		1	1	Va	Va	Va	

Name	Color	Sex	Age	Month of Birth	Relationship	Marital Status	Married During Year	Occupation	Months Unem- ployed	Sickness Blind Deaf & Dumb Idiotic Disabled
Dwelling #120/Family #121										
Frances E. Wright	W	F	45			W		Keeping house		
John W. Wright	W	M	26		Son	S		Farm Laborer		
Victoria A. Wright	W	F	24		Daughter	S		No occupation		
Dwelling #248/Family #250										
Lankford Wright	B	M	45			M		Farm laborer		
Emily Wright	B	F	40		Wife	M		Keeping house		
Mary F. Wright	B	F	17		daughter	S		at Home		
Nannie Wright	B	F	13		daughter	S		at Home		
Rosey Wright	B	F	11		daughter	S		at Home		
Pinkard Wright	B	M	8		Son	S				
Emma Wright	B	F	2		Granddaughter	S				
Nannie Wright	B	F	6/12	Nov	Granddaughter	S				

Little Creek District
3 day of June, 1880

Name	Color	Sex	Age	Month of Birth	Relationship	Marital Status	Married During Year	Occupation	Months Unem- ployed	Sickness Blind Deaf & Dumb Idiotic Disabled
Dwelling #29/Family #29										
Joshua Wright	Mu	M	55			M		Farmer		
Sarah A. Wright	Mu	F	58		Wife	M		Keeping house		

Appendix: Franklin County, Virginia, 1880 Census

Name continued from previous page]	Attended School Within Year	Cannot Read	Cannot Write	Born	Father Born	Mother Born	Identification
Dwelling #120/Family #121							
Frances E. Wright				Virginia	Va	Va	Elizabeth Frances (Cundiff) Wright, widow of 1862 Abraham O.
John W. Wright		1	1	Virginia	Va	Va	Wright of Franklin County, a son of 1883 Anslem Wright of
Victoria A. Wright		1	1	Virginia	Va	Va	Franklin County and grandson of William Wright
Dwelling #248/Family #250							
Lankford Wright		1	1	Va	Va	Va	Lankford Wright, son of Tandy Graves
Emily Wright		1	1	Va	Va	Va	
Mary F. Wright	1		1	Va	Va	Va	
Nannie Wright	1	1	1	Va	Va	Va	
Rosey Wright	1	1	1	Va	Va	Va	
Pinkard Wright				Va	Va	Va	
Emma Wright				Va	Va	Va	
Nannie Wright				Va	Va	Va	

Little Creek District
3 day of June, 1880

Dwelling #29/Family #29							
Joshua Wright		1	1	Virginia	Va	Va	
Sarah A. Wright		1	1	Virginia	Va	Va	

Name	Color	Sex	Age	Month of Birth	Relationship	Marital Status	Married During Year	Occupation	Months Unemployed	Sickness Blind Deaf & Dumb Idiotic Disabled

3d & 4th day of June, 1880

Dwelling #44/Family #44

Name	Color	Sex	Age	Month of Birth	Relationship	Marital Status	Married During Year	Occupation	Months Unemployed	Sickness Blind Deaf & Dumb Idiotic Disabled
Otey Wright	W	M	52			M		Farmer		
Caroline Wright	W	F	64		Wife	M		Keeping House		
Misura Wright	W	F	13		Daughter	S		at Home		
Chas Wright	W	M	12		Son	S		Working on Farm		
Thos Wright	W	M	10		Son	S		working on Farm		
James Wright	W	M	8		Son	S				
Wm Wright	W	M	6		Son	S				
Dandrige Wright	W	M	2		Son	S				
Infant Wright	W	F	4/12		Daughter	S				

Dwelling #49/Family #49

Name	Color	Sex	Age	Month of Birth	Relationship	Marital Status	Married During Year	Occupation	Months Unemployed	Sickness Blind Deaf & Dumb Idiotic Disabled
Wm Wright	W	M	58					Farmer		
Maria Wright	W	F	28		Wife	M		Keeping House		
Althea S. Wright	W	F	6		Daughter	S				
Wm J. Wright	W	M	3		Son	S				
James M. Wright	W	M	2		Son	S				
Elizabeth Webb	W	F	50		Boarder	S		No occupation		
Sydna Webb	W	M	15		Boarder	S		No occupation		
Mary Nunley	W	F	18		Boarder			No occupation		

Dwelling #67/Family #67

Name	Color	Sex	Age	Month of Birth	Relationship	Marital Status	Married During Year	Occupation	Months Unemployed	Sickness Blind Deaf & Dumb Idiotic Disabled
John W. Abshire	W	M	27			S		Farmer		
Peter Wright	W	M	26		Tennant(?)	S		working on Farm		
James Abshire	W	M	25		Brother	S		working on Farm		

Name continued from previous page]	Attended School Within Year	Cannot Read	Cannot Write	Born	Father Born	Mother Born	Identification
3d & 4th day of June, 1880							
Dwelling #44/Family #44							
Otey Wright				Virginia	Va	Va	1918 Otey Wright of Franklin County, son of 1839 John A.
Caroline Wright				Virginia	Va	Va	Wright of Franklin County, grandson of 1830 William Wright of
Misura Wright				Virginia	Va	Va	Franklin County, great grandson of 1809 William Wright of
Chas Wright				Virginia	Va	Va	Franklin County, and probably great great grandson of 1792
Thos Wright		1	1	Virginia	Va	Va	John Wright of Fauquier County
James Wright				Virginia	Va	Va	
Wm Wright				Virginia	Va	Va	
Dandrige Wright				Virginia	Va	Va	
Infant Wright				Virginia	Va	Va	
Dwelling #49/Family #49							
Wm Wright		1	1	Virginia	Va	Va	William H. Wright, son of 1839 John A. Wright of Franklin
Maria Wright				Virginia	Va	Va	County, grandson of 1830 William Wright of Franklin County,
Althea S. Wright				Virginia	Va	Va	great grandson of 1809 William Wright of Franklin County,
Wm J. Wright				Virginia	Va	Va	and probably great great grandson of 1792 John Wright of
James M. Wright				Virginia	Va	Va	Fauquier County
Elizabeth Webb				Virginia	Va	Va	
Sydna Webb		1	1	Virginia	Va	Va	
Mary Nunley		1	1	Virginia	Va	Va	
Dwelling #67/Family #67							
John W. Abshire				Virginia	Va	Va	
Peter Wright				Virginia	Va	Va	
James Abshire							

Name	Color	Sex	Age	Monthof Birth	Relationship	Marital Status	Married During Year	Occupation	Months Unem- ployed	Sickness Blind Deaf & Dumb Idiotic Disabled

7th day of June, 1880

Dwelling #94/Family #94

Name	Color	Sex	Age	Monthof Birth	Relationship	Marital Status	Married During Year	Occupation	Months Unem- ployed	Sickness Blind Deaf & Dumb Idiotic Disabled
Jno A. Wright	W	M	62			M		Farmer		
Mary E. Wright	W	F	51		Wife	M		Keeping House		
Jno M. Wright	W	M	27		Son	S		working on Farm		
Sarah Pearson	W	M	40		Sister in law	S				
James Wright	W	M	17			S				

Dwelling #103/Family #104

Name	Color	Sex	Age	Monthof Birth	Relationship	Marital Status	Married During Year	Occupation	Months Unem- ployed	Sickness Blind Deaf & Dumb Idiotic Disabled
Wm Beckner	W	M				S		Farmer		
Permelia Beckner	W	F			Mother	W		Keeps house		
Permelia Wright	W	F			Boarder	S		without occupation		
Margaret Wright	W	F			Boarder	S		without occupation		
George Gustine	W	M				S		works on farm		
E J Wright	W	F	11		Boarder	S		no occupation		

Dwelling #136/Family #138

Name	Color	Sex	Age	Monthof Birth	Relationship	Marital Status	Married During Year	Occupation	Months Unem- ployed	Sickness Blind Deaf & Dumb Idiotic Disabled
J. G. Wright	W		46			M		Farmer		
Polly Wright	W		36		Wife	M		Keeping House		
Wilson Mills	W		18		Servant	S		working on Farm		
Arrena Mills	W		25		Sister-in-law	S		At Home		
Tena Mills	W		79		Mother-in-law	M		At Home		

Appendix: Franklin County, Virginia, 1880 Census

Name continued from previous page]	Attended School Within Year	Cannot Read	Cannot Write	Born	Father Born	Mother Born	Identification
7th day of June, 1880							
Dwelling #94/Family #94							
Jno A. Wright				Virginia	Va	Va	1905 John A. Wright of Franklin County, son of 1843 George
Mary E. Wright				Virginia	Va	Va	Wright of Franklin County,grandson of 1809 William Wright
Jno M. Wright				Virginia	Va	Va	of Franklin County, and probably great grandson of 1792 John
Sarah Pearson				Virginia	Va	Va	Wright of Fauquier County
James Wright			1	Virginia	Va	Va	
Dwelling #103/Family #104							
Wm Beckner				Virginia	Va	Va	Permelia A. (Wright) Beckner, and Margaret Wright, daughters
Permelia Beckner		1	1	Virginia	Va	Va	of James Grant Wright, Sr., granddaughters of 1823 James
Permelia Wright				Virginia	Va	Va	Wright of Franklin County, great granddaughters of 1809
Margaret Wright				Virginia	Va	Va	William Wright of Franklin County, and probably great great
George Gustine	1	1	1	Virginia	Va	Va	granddaughters of 1792 John Wright of Fauquier County
E J Wright		1	1	Virginia	Va	Va	
Dwelling #136/Family #138							
J. G. Wright				Virginia	Va	Va	1905 James G. Wright of Franklin County, son of 1896 John B.
Polly Wright				Virginia	Va	Va	Wright of Franklin County, grandson of 1823 James Wright of
Wilson Mills		1	1	Virginia	Va	Va	Franklin County, great grandson of 1809 William Wright of
Arrena Mills				Virginia	Va	Va	Franklin County, and probably great great grandson of 1792
Tena Mills				Virginia	Va	Va	John Wright of Fauquier County

Name	Color	Sex	Age	Monthof Birth	Relationship	Marital Status	Married During Year	Occupation	Months Unem- ployed	Sickness Blind Deaf & Dumb Idiotic Disabled

16th day of June, 1880

Dwelling #234/Family #236

Name	Color	Sex	Age	Monthof Birth	Relationship	Marital Status	Married During Year	Occupation	Months Unem- ployed	Sickness Blind Deaf & Dumb Idiotic Disabled
Judith P. Wright	W	F	62			W		Farmer		
J.E.M. Wright	W	M	33		Son	S		works on Farm		
Thomas H. Wright	W	M	29		Son	S		works on Farm		

Appendix: Franklin County, Virginia, 1880 Census

Name continued from previous page]	Attended School Within Year	Cannot Read	Cannot Write	Born	Father Born	Mother Born	Identification
16th day of June, 1880							
Dwelling #234/Family #236							
Judith P. Wright				Virginia	Va	Va	Judith P. (Wright) Wright, daughter of 1855 Wright Wright of
J.E.M. Wright				Virginia	Va	Va	Franklin County, granddaughter of 1815 Joseph Wright of
Thomas H. Wright				Virginia	Va	Va	Franklin County, and great granddaughter of 1763 Thomas
							Wright of Bedford County and widow of 1877 James Wright of
							Franklin County, a son of 1850 Tommey Wright of Bedford
							County, grandson of 1803 John Wright of Bedford County, and
							great grandson of 1763 Thomas Wright of Bedford County

1900 CENSUS

FRANKLIN COUNTY, VIRGINIA

Appendix: Franklin County, Virginia, 1900 Census

Location				Relation	Personal Description									
In Cities	Number of dwelling houses in the order of visitation	Number of family in the order of visitation	Name of each person whose place of abode on June 1, 1900, was in this family.	Relation-ship of each person to the head the family	Color or race	Sex	Date of Birth Month	Year	Age at last birth-day	Whether single, married, widowed, or divorced	Number of years married	Mother of how many children	Number of these children living	
Street / House Number														

Blackwater District

	Number of dwelling houses	Number of family	Name	Relation	Color or race	Sex	Month	Year	Age	Whether single, married, etc.	Number of years married	Mother of how many children	Number of these children living
	172	173	Francis Dillars	Head	B	F	Apl	1860	40	M	25	9	9
			Will Dillars	Son	B	M	Aug	1885	14	S			
			Annie Dillars	Daughter	B	F	May	1888	12	S			
			Charly Dillars	Son	B	M	Oct	1890	9	S			
			Lizzie Dillars	Daughter	B	F	Aug	1892	7	S			
			Johnnie Dillars	Son	B	M	Apr	1896	6	S			
			Ula Dillars	Daughter	B	F	Feb	1898	2	S			
			Allie Wright	Daughter	B	F	Jan	1883	17	S		1	1
			Harris Wright	Gran Dau	B	M	Mar	1899	1	S			
	203	204	George A. Wright	Head	W	M	Sep	1861	38	M	21		
			Elizabeth A. Wright	Wife	W	F	Jul	1855	45	M	21	7	6
			Mary E. Wright	Daughtr	W	F	Dec	1879	20	S			
			Evvie G. Wright	Daughtr	W	F	Jun	1882	17	S			
			Chester A. Wright	Son	W	M	July	1884	15	S			
			Olivia W. Wright	Daughtr	W	F	Jan	1891	9	S			
			Sid L. M. Wright	Son	W	M	Feb	1894	6	S			
			William M. Wright	Son	W	M	Sept	1896	3	S			
			Oney Bryant	Aunt	W	F	Apr	1826	74	S			
	208	209	Jacob A. Wright	Head	W	M	Dec	1871	28	M	6		
			Clarry Wright	Wife	W	F	July	1861	39	M	6	2	1
			Jacob L. Wright	Son	W	M	Apr	1895	5	S			
			Sarah J. Coops	Friend(?)	W	F	Mar	1827	73	S			

Appendix: Franklin County, Virginia, 1900 Census

| Name of each person whose place of abode on June 1, 1900, was in this family. [continued from prior page] | Nativity | | | Citizenship | | | Occupation, Trade, Or Profession of each person Ten Years of age and over. | | Education | | |
	Place of birth of this Person	Place of birth of Father of this person	Place of birth of Mother of this person	Year of immigration to the United States	Number of years in the United States	Natural-ization	Occupation	Months not employed	Attended school in months)	Can read	Can write	Can speak English
Blackwater District												
Francis Dillars	Virginia	Virginia	Virginia				Farm			yes	no	yes
Will Dillars	Virginia	Virginia	Virginia				Farm Labor	3		no	no	yes
Annie Dillars	Virginia	Virginia	Virginia					3		yes	yes	yes
Charly Dillars	Virginia	Virginia	Virginia					3				
Lizzie Dillars	Virginia	Virginia	Virginia					0				
Johnnie Dillars	Virginia	Virginia	Virginia					0				
Ula Dillars	Virginia	Virginia	Virginia									
Allie Wright	Virginia	Virginia	Virginia							yes	yes	yes
Harris Wright	Virginia	Virginia	Virginia									
George A. Wright	Virginia	Virginia	Virginia				Farm			Yes	Yes	Yes
Elizabeth A. Wright	Virginia	Virginia	Virginia							Yes	Yes	Yes
Mary E. Wright	Virginia	Virginia	Virginia				School teacher	7	0	Yes	Yes	Yes
Evvie G. Wright	Virginia	Virginia	Virginia							Yes	Yes	Yes
Chester A. Wright	Virginia	Virginia	Virginia				Farm labor	0	0	Yes	Yes	Yes
Olivia W. Wright	Virginia	Virginia	Virginia						4			
Sid L. M. Wright	Virginia	Virginia	Virginia						4			
William M. Wright	Virginia	Virginia	Virginia									
Oney Bryant	Virginia	Virginia	Virginia									
Jacob A. Wright	Virginia	Virginia	Virginia				Farmer			Yes	Yes	Yes
Clarry Wright	Virginia	Virginia	Virginia							Yes	Yes	Yes
Jacob L. Wright	Virginia	Virginia	Virginia									
Sarah J. Coops	Virginia	Virginia	Virginia									

Appendix: Franklin County, Virginia, 1900 Census

Ownership Of Home

Name of each person whose place of abode on June 1, 1900, was in this family. [continued from prior page]	Owned or rented	Owned free or mortgaged	Farm or house	Number of farm schedule	Identification
Blackwater District					
Francis Dillars	R		H		
Will Dillars					
Annie Dillars					
Charly Dillars					
Lizzie Dillars					
Johnnie Dillars					
Ula Dillars					
Allie Wright					
Harris Wright					
George A. Wright	O	F	F	163	1954 George A. Wright of Franklin County, son of 1901 Crockett Anderson Wright of Franklin County and grandson of Smith Wright (Montgomery County)
Elizabeth A. Wright					
Mary E. Wright					
Evvie G. Wright					
Chester A. Wright					
Olivia W. Wright					
Sid L. M. Wright					
William M. Wright					
Oney Bryant					
Jacob A. Wright	R		F	68	1960 Jacob Anderson Wright, son of 1918 Isaac M. Wright of Franklin County, grandson of 1901 Crockett Anderson Wright of Franklin County, and great grandson of Smith Wright (Montgomery County)
Clarry Wright					
Jacob L. Wright					
Sarah J. Coops					

	Location				Relation				Personal Description						
					Relation-ship of								Whether single,			Number
		Number of dwelling	Number of family	Name of each	each							Age at	married,			of these
In Cities		houses in	in the	person whose place of	person							last	widowed,	Number	Mother of	children
	House	the order of	order of	abode on June 1, 1900,	to the head	Color			Date of Birth		birth-	or	of years	how many	children
Street	Number	visitation	visitation	was in this family.	the family	or race	Sex	Month	Year	day	divorced	married	children	living
		209	210	Isaac M. Wright	Head	W	M	Nov	1848	51	M	28		
				Oney Wright	Wife	W	F	Jan	1847	53	M	28	10	9
				Lucy E. Wright	Daughter	W	F	Nov	1875	24	S			
				Kicheny Wright	Daughter	W	F	May	1877	23	S			
				Isaac M. Wright Jr.	Son	W	M	June	1878	21	S			
				Weaklie J. Wright	Son	W	M	July	1880	19	S			
				Oney L. Wright	Daughter	W	F	Mar	1884	16	S			
				Geneva Wright	Daughter	W	F	Apr	1886	14	S			
		246	247	Henry C. Wright	Head	W	M	May	1874	26	M	0		
				Dasie C. Wright	Wife	W	F	Nov	1880	19	M	0	0	0
		273	274	Joel T Wright	Head	W	M	April	1864	36	M	12		
				Martha F Wright	Wife	W	F	Sept	1873	26	M	12	7	7
				Monldee E. Wright	Daughter	W	F	April	1889	11	S			
				Richard D. Wright	Son	W	M	Nov	1890	9	S			
				Ruth E. Wright	Daughter	W	F	June	1892	7	S			
				Brad B. Wright	Son	W	M	April	1894	6	S			
				Isaac C. Wright	Son	W	M	June	1896	3	S			
				Dewie D. Wright	Son	W	M	Apri	1898	2	S			
				Not named Wright	Son	W	M	Aug	1899	1/12	S			

Name of each person whose place of abode on June 1, 1900, was in this family. [continued from prior page]	Nativity			Citizenship			Occupation, Trade, Or Profession of each person Ten Years of age and over.		Education			
	Place of birth of each person and parents of each person enumerated.			Year of immigration to the United States	Number of years in the United States	Natural-ization		Months not employed	Attended school in months)	Can read	Can write	Can speak English
	Place of birth of this Person	Place of birth of Father of this person	Place of birth of Mother of this person				Occupation					
Isaac M. Wright	Virginia	Virginia	Virginia				Farmer	0		Yes	Yes	Yes
Oney Wright	Virginia	Virginia	Virginia							Yes	No	Yes
Lucy E. Wright	Virginia	Virginia	Virginia							Yes	Yes	Yes
Kicheny Wright	Virginia	Virginia	Virginia							Yes	Yes	Yes
Isaac M. Wright Jr.	Virginia	Virginia	Virginia							Yes	Yes	Yes
Weaklie J. Wright	Virginia	Virginia	Virginia				Farm Laborer	0	2	Yes	Yes	Yes
Oney L. Wright	Virginia	Virginia	Virginia				Farm Laborer	0	4	Yes	Yes	Yes
Geneva Wright	Virginia	Virginia	Virginia						4	Yes	Yes	Yes
Henry C. Wright	Virginia	Virginia	Virginia				Farmer	0		Yes	Yes	Yes
Dasie C. Wright	Virginia	Virginia	Virginia						0	Yes	Yes	Yes
Joel T Wright	Virginia	Virginia	Virginia				Farmer	0		Yes	Yes	Yes
Martha F Wright	Virginia	Virginia	Virginia							Yes	Yes	Yes
Monldee E. Wright	Virginia	Virginia	Virginia						4			
Richard D. Wright	Virginia	Virginia	Virginia						4	No	No	No
Ruth E. Wright	Virginia	Virginia	Virginia						0			
Brad B. Wright	Virginia	Virginia	Virginia						0			
Isaac C. Wright	Virginia	Virginia	Virginia									
Dewie D. Wright	Virginia	Virginia	Virginia									
Not named Wright	Virginia	Virginia	Virginia									

Ownership Of Home

Name of each person whose place of abode on June 1, 1900, was in this family. [continued from prior page]	Owned or rented	Owned free or mortgaged	Farm or house	Number of farm schedule	Identification
Isaac M. Wright Oney Wright Lucy E. Wright Kicheny Wright Isaac M. Wright Jr. Weaklie J. Wright Oney L. Wright Geneva Wright	0	F	F	69	1918 Isaac M. Wright of Franklin County, son of 1901 Crockett Anderson Wright of Franklin County and grandson of Smith Wright (Montgomery County)
Henry C. Wright Dasie C. Wright	O	M	F	200	1929 Henry Crocket Wright of Franklin County, son of 1918 Isaac M. Wright of Franklin County, grandson of 1901 Crockett Anderson Wright of Franklin County, and great grandson of Smith Wright (Montgomery County)
Joel T Wright Martha F Wright Monldee E. Wright Richard D. Wright Ruth E. Wright Brad B. Wright Isaac C. Wright Dewie D. Wright Not named Wright	R		F	219	1932 Joel Thomas Wright of Franklin County, son of 1901 Crockett Anderson Wright of Franklin County and grandson of Smith Wright (Montgomery County)

	Location				Relation				Personal Description						
		Number of dwelling houses in the order of	Number of family in the order of	Name of each person whose place of abode on June 1, 1900,	Relation-ship of each person to the head	Color		Date of Birth		Age at last birth-	Whether single, married, widowed, or	Number of years	Mother of how many	Number of these children
In Cities															
Street	House Number	the order of visitation	order of visitation	was in this family.	the family	or race	Sex	Month	Year	day	divorced	married	children	living
		275	276	Benjamin C Wright	Head	W	M	May	1859	41	M	20		
				Arkansas Wright	Wife	W	F	July	1858	41	M	20	9	8
				James K. Wright	Son	W	M	June	1881	18	S			
				Noah S. Wright	Son	W	M	May	1883	17	S			
				Harriet A. Wright	Daughter	W	F	Nov	1886	13	S			
				Emily E. Wright	Daughter	W	F	May	1889	11	S			
				Ferdersie A. Wright	Daughter	W	F	July	1891	8	S			
				Isaac Grant Wright	Son	W	M	Sept	1894	5	S			
				Oney F. Wright	Daughter	W	F	Oct	1896	3	S			
				Jessie C. Wright	Son	W	M	May	1899	1	S			
		281	282	Crockett Wright	Head	W	M	Aug	1828	71	W			
				Serena Wright	Daughter	W	F	Oct	1854	45	S			
				Rufus Wright	Grandson	W	M	May	1879	21	S			
		287	288	Nancy E. Wright	Head	W	F	Oct	1856	43	W		10	9
				John W Wright	Son	W	M	Feb	1883	17	S			
				Jennie Wright	Daughter	W	F	Mar	1884	16	S			
				Mollie Wright	Daughter	W	F	Aug	1887	12	S			
				Alis C. Wright	Daughter	W	F	Jan	1888	11	S			
				Birta Wright	Daughter	W	F	May	1890	10	S			
				Minnie Wright	Daughter	W	F	Apr	1895	4	S			
				Thos A. Wright	Son	W	M	April	1897	3	S			

Name of each person whose place of abode on June 1, 1900, was in this family. [continued from prior page]	Nativity — Place of birth of each person and parents of each person enumerated.			Citizenship			Occupation, Trade, Or Profession of each person Ten Years of age and over.		Education			
	Place of birth of this Person	Place of birth of Father of this person	Place of birth of Mother of this person	Year of immigration to the United States	Number of years in the United States	Natural-ization	Occupation	Months not employed	Attended school in months)	Can read	Can write	Can speak English
Benjamin C Wright	Virginia	Virginia	Virginia				Farmer	0		Yes	Yes	Yes
Arkansas Wright	Virginia	Virginia	Virginia							No	No	Yes
James K. Wright	Virginia	Virginia	Virginia				Farm laborer	0	0	Yes	Yes	Yes
Noah S. Wright	Virginia	Virginia	Virginia				Farm laborer	0	0	Yes	No	Yes
Harriet A. Wright	Virginia	Virginia	Virginia						4	Yes	Yes	Yes
Emily E. Wright	Virginia	Virginia	Virginia						4	Yes	Yes	Yes
Ferdersie A. Wright	Virginia	Virginia	Virginia						4			
Isaac Grant Wright	Virginia	Virginia	Virginia						0			
Oney F. Wright	Virginia	Virginia	Virginia									
Jessie C. Wright	Virginia	Virginia	Virginia									
Crockett Wright	Virginia	Virginia	Virginia				Blacksmith	0		Yes	No	Yes
Serena Wright	Virginia	Virginia	Virginia							No	No	Yes
Rufus Wright	Virginia	Virginia	Virginia				Farm labr	0		Yes	No	Yes
Nancy E. Wright	Virginia	Virginia	Virginia				Farm	0		Yes	Yes	Yes
John W Wright	Virginia	Virginia	Virginia				Farm Laborer	0		No	No	Yes
Jennie Wright	Virginia	Virginia	Virginia							Yes	No	Yes
Mollie Wright	Virginia	Virginia	Virginia							No	No	Yes
Alis C. Wright	Virginia	Virginia	Virginia							No	No	Yes
Birta Wright	Virginia	Virginia	Virginia							No	No	Yes
Minnie Wright	Virginia	Virginia	Virginia									
Thos A. Wright	Virginia	Virginia	Virginia									

Name of each person whose place of abode on June 1, 1900, was in this family. [continued from prior page]	Ownership Of Home				Identification
	Owned or rented	Owned free or mortgaged	Farm or house	Number of farm schedule	
Benjamin C Wright Arkansas Wright James K. Wright Noah S. Wright Harriet A. Wright Emily E. Wright Ferdersie A. Wright Isaac Grant Wright Oney F. Wright Jessie C. Wright	O	F	F	221	1925 William Benjamin C. Wright of Franklin County, son of 1901 Crockett Anderson Wright of Franklin County and grandson of Smith Wright (Montgomery County)
Crockett Wright Serena Wright Rufus Wright	R		H	17	1901 Crockett Anderson Wright of Franklin County, son of Smith Wright (Montgomery County)
Nancy E. Wright John W Wright Jennie Wright Mollie Wright Alis C. Wright Birta Wright Minnie Wright Thos A. Wright	R		F	228	Nancy E. (Saul) Wright, widow of John Henry Wright, a son of 1901 Crockett Anderson Wright of Franklin County and grandson of Smith Wright (Montgomery County)

Appendix: Franklin County, Virginia, 1900 Census

	Location				Relation			Personal Description						
In Cities Street	House Number	Number of dwelling houses in the order of visitation	Number of family in the order of visitation	Name of each person whose place of abode on June 1, 1900, was in this family.	Relation-ship of each person to the head the family	Color or race	Sex	Date of Birth Month	Year	Age at last birth-day	Whether single, married, widowed, or divorced	Number of years married	Mother of how many children	Number of these children living
		21	21	Thomas M Wright	Head	W	M	Apr	1870	30	M	4		
				Gustavus Wright	Wife	W	F	Apr	1874	26	M	4	2	2
				Recie H. Wright	Daughter	W	F	Aug	1897	2				
		20	20	Otey Wright	Head	W	M	Sept	1828	71	M	10		
				Lucinda Wright	Wife	W	F	June	1836	68	M	10	3	3
				William O. Wright	Son	W	M	Oct	1875	24	S			
				Dandrige A. Wright	Son	W	M	May	1877	23	S			

Bonbrook District

In Cities Street	House Number	Number of dwelling houses in the order of visitation	Number of family in the order of visitation	Name of each person whose place of abode on June 1, 1900, was in this family.	Relation-ship of each person to the head the family	Color or race	Sex	Date of Birth Month	Year	Age at last birth-day	Whether single, married, widowed, or divorced	Number of years married	Mother of how many children	Number of these children living
		22	22	Charles Wright	Head	W	M	Oct	1867	32	M	8		
				Fanny Wright	Wife	W	F	Dec	1871	28	M	8	3	3
				Frank N. Wright	Son	W	M	Aug	1894	5	S			
				George O. Wright	Son	W	M	Oct	1896	3	S			
				Ethel C. Wright	Daughter	W	F	Dec	1899	5/12	S			
				Eldrige Wright	Boarder	W	M	Nov	1898	1	S			
		50	59	Asa Wright	Head	W	M	March	1816	84	Wd			

Appendix: Franklin County, Virginia, 1900 Census

Name of each person whose place of abode on June 1, 1900, was in this family. [continued from prior page]	Nativity			Citizenship			Occupation, Trade, Or Profession of each person Ten Years of age and over.		Education			
	Place of birth of each person and parents of each person enumerated.											
	Place of birth of this Person	Place of birth of Father of this person	Place of birth of Mother of this person	Year of immi- gration to the United States	Number of years in the United States	Natural- ization	Occupation	Months not employed	Attended school in months)	Can read	Can write	Can speak English
Thomas M Wright	Virginia	Virginia	Virginia				Farmer	0		Yes	Yes	Yes
Gustavus Wright	Virginia	Virginia	Virginia							Yes	Yes	Yes
Recie H. Wright	Virginia	Virginia	Virginia									
Otey Wright	Virginia	Virginia	Virginia				Farmer	0		Yes	Yes	Yes
Lucinda Wright	Virginia	Virginia	Virginia							Yes	Yes	Yes
William O. Wright	Virginia	Virginia	Virginia				Farm laborer	0		Yes	Yes	Yes
Dandrige A. Wright	Virginia	Virginia	Virginia				RR section laborer	0		Yes	Yes	Yes

Bonbrook District

Name												
Charles Wright	Virginia	Virginia	Virginia				Farmer	0		Yes	Yes	Yes
Fanny Wright	Virginia	Virginia	Virginia							Yes	Yes	Yes
Frank N. Wright	Virginia	Virginia	Virginia						0			
George O. Wright	Virginia	Virginia	Virginia									
Ethel C. Wright	Virginia	Virginia	Virginia									
Eldrige Wright	Virginia	Virginia	Virginia									
Asa Wright	Virginia	Virginia	Virginia				Landlord			Yes	Yes	Yes

Ownership Of Home

Name of each person whose place of abode on June 1, 1900, was in this family. [continued from prior page]	Owned or rented	Owned free or mortgaged	Farm or house	Number of farm schedule	Identification
Thomas M Wright Gustavus Wright Recie H. Wright	R		F	18	1944 Thomas N. Wright of Franklin County, son of 1918 Otey Wright of Franklin County, grandson of 1839 John A. Wright of Franklin County, great grandson of 1830 William Wright of Franklin County, great great grandson of 1809 William Wright of Franklin County, and probably great great great grandson of 1792 John Wright of Fauquier County
Otey Wright Lucinda Wright William O. Wright Dandrige A. Wright	O	F	F	17	1918 Otey Wright of Franklin County, son of 1839 John A. Wright of Franklin County, grandson of 1830 William Wright of Franklin County, and great grandson of 1809 William Wright of Franklin County, and probably great great grandson of 1792 John Wright of Fauquier County

Bonbrook District

Charles Wright Fanny Wright Frank N. Wright George O. Wright Ethel C. Wright Eldrige Wright	O	F	F	19	Charles H. Wright, son of 1918 Otey Wright of Franklin County, grandson of 1839 John A. Wright of Franklin County, great grandson of 1830 William Wright of Franklin County, and great great grandson of 1809 William Wright of Franklin County, and probably great great great grandson of 1792 John Wright of Fauquier County
Asa Wright	O		H		1901 Asa Wright of Franklin County, son of 1839 John A. Wright of Franklin County, grandson of 1830 William Wright of Franklin County, and great grandson of 1809 William Wright of Franklin County, and probably great great grandson of 1792 John Wright of Fauquier County

Appendix: Franklin County, Virginia, 1900 Census

	Location				Relation			Personal Description						
		Number of dwelling houses in the order of visitation	Number of family in the order of visitation	Name of each person whose place of abode on June 1, 1900, was in this family.	Relationship of each person to the head the family	Color or race	Sex	Date of Birth		Age at last birthday	Whether single, married, widowed, or divorced	Number of years married	Mother of how many children	Number of these children living
In Cities								Month	Year					
Street	House Number													
		76	76	John W. Wright	Head	B	M	Apr	1845	55	M	34		
				Catharine Wright	Wife	B	F	Apr	1845	55	M	34	15	10
				Edmund Wright	Son	B	M	Dec	1885	14	S			
				Henrietta Wright	Daughter	B	F	Nov	1886	13	S			
				Berta Wright	Daughter	B	F	Apr	1891	9	S			
				Julia Wright	Mother	B	F	Dec	1822	77	Wd			
				Joel Price	Boarder	B	M	July	1832	67	Wd			
				Henry Childress	Boarder	B	M	Sept	1882	17	S			
		91	91	William T Wright	Head	W	M	July	1840	60	M	38		
				Octava M Wright	Wife	W	F	Sept	1842	57	M	38	8	6
				James C. Wright	Son	W	M	March	1875	25	S			
		24	24	McGeorge M. Wright	Head	W	M	Jul	1852	47	M	11		
				Deborah J. Wright	Wife	W	F	Mar	1871	29	M	11	7	6
				Carrol W. Wright	Son	W	M	Feb	1890	10	S			
				Eva E. Wright	Daughter	W	F	Jul	1891	8	S			
				Willie M Wright	Daughter	W	F	Feb	1893	7	S			
				Callie M. Wright	Daughter	W	F	Jan	1895	5	S			
				Dalton C. Wright	Son	W	M	Nov	1897	2	S			
				Ida S. Wright	Daughter	W	F	Dec	1899	5/12	S			

Appendix: Franklin County, Virginia, 1900 Census

Name of each person whose place of abode on June 1, 1900, was in this family. [continued from prior page]	Nativity			Citizenship			Occupation, Trade, Or Profession of each person Ten Years of age and over.		Education			
	Place of birth of each person and parents of each person enumerated.											
	Place of birth of this Person	Place of birth of Father of this person	Place of birth of Mother of this person	Year of immi- gration to the United States	Number of years in the United States	Natural- ization	Occupation	Months not employed	Attended school in months)	Can read	Can write	Can speak English
John W. Wright	Virginia	Virginia	Virginia				Farmer	0		Yes	No	Yes
Catharine Wright	Virginia	Virginia	Virginia							No	No	Yes
Edmund Wright	Virginia	Virginia	Virginia				At School		3	Yes	Yes	Yes
Henrietta Wright	Virginia	Virginia	Virginia				At School		3	Yes	Yes	Yes
Berta Wright	Virginia	Virginia	Virginia				At School		3	Yes	Yes	Yes
Julia Wright	Virginia	Virginia	Virginia									
Joel Price	Virginia	Virginia	Virginia				Farm laborer	6		No	No	Yes
Henry Childress	Virginia	Virginia	Virginia				At School		2	No	No	Yes
William T Wright	Virginia	Virginia	Virginia				Farmer	0		Yes	Yes	Yes
Octava M Wright	Virginia	Virginia	Virginia							Yes	Yes	Yes
James C. Wright	Virginia	Virginia	Virginia				Farm laborer	0		Yes	Yes	Yes
McGeorge M. Wright	Virginia	Virginia	Virginia				Farmer	0		Yes	Yes	Yes
Deborah J. Wright	Virginia	Virginia	Virginia							Yes	Yes	Yes
Carrol W. Wright	Virginia	Virginia	Virginia				Farm laborer	0		Yes	Yes	Yes
Eva E. Wright	Virginia	Virginia	Virginia									
Willie M Wright	Virginia	Virginia	Virginia									
Callie M. Wright	Virginia	Virginia	Virginia									
Dalton C. Wright	Virginia	Virginia	Virginia									
Ida S. Wright	Virginia	Virginia	Virginia									

Appendix: Franklin County, Virginia, 1900 Census

_____Ownership Of Home_____

Name of each person whose place of abode on June 1, 1900, was in this family. [continued from prior page]	Owned or rented	Owned free or mortgaged	Farm or house	Number of farm schedule	Identification
John W. Wright Catharine Wright Edmund Wright Henrietta Wright Berta Wright Julia Wright Joel Price Henry Childress	R		F	63	John Wesley Wright, son of Joshua Wright
William T Wright Octava M Wright James C. Wright	O	F	F	77	1928 William T. Wright, son of 1890 Robert Penn Wright of Franklin County, grandson of 1849 Thomas Wright of Franklin County, great grandson of 1815 Joseph Wright of Bedford County and great grandson of 1803 John Wright of Bedford County, and great great grandson of 1763 Thomas Wright of Bedford County
McGeorge M. Wright Deborah J. Wright Carrol W. Wright Eva E. Wright Willie M Wright Callie M. Wright Dalton C. Wright Ida S. Wright	O	F	F	20	1934 Milton McGeorge Wright of Franklin County, son of 1890 Robert Penn Wright of Franklin County, grandson of 1849 Thomas Wright of Franklin County, great grandson of 1815 Joseph Wright of Bedford County and great grandson of 1803 John Wright of Bedford County, and great great grandson of 1763 Thomas Wright of Bedford County

Location						**Relation**				**Personal Description**					
In Cities		Number of dwelling houses in the order of visitation	Number of family in the order of visitation	Name of each person whose place of abode on June 1, 1900, was in this family.	Relationship of each person to the head the family	Color or race	Sex	Date of Birth Month	Year	Age at last birthday	Whether single, married, widowed, or divorced	Number of years married	Mother of how many children	Number of these children living
Street	House Number													
		29	29	Cicero A. Wright	Head	W	M	May	1856	44	M	4		
				Gertrude Wright	Wife	W	F	July	1876	23	M	4	2	2
				Mable C. Wright	Daughter	W	F	Mar	1896	3	S			
				Herbert M. Wright	Son	W	M	Feb	1900	3/12	S			

Gills Creek District

Number of dwelling houses	Number of family	Name of each person	Relationship to head	Color or race	Sex	Month	Year	Age	Whether single/married	Number of years married	Mother of how many children	Number of these children living
27	27	Nelly(?) L Starky	Head	B	F	Mar	1871	26	S	3	3	
		Robert I Starky	Son	B	M	Sep	1893	6	S			
		Lucy J Starky	Daughter	B	F	Dec	1895	4	S			
		James H. Starky	Son	B	M	July	1899	11/12	S			
		Florence Wright	Servant	B	F	June	1880	20	S			
33	33	John D Hannabas	Head	W	M	Oct	1864	35	M	10		
		Jammima(?) Hannabas	Wife	W	F	Nov	1869	30	M	10	1	1
		Ola M Hannabas	Daughter	W	F	Feb	1892	8	S			
		Fleming Wright	Boarder	W	M	Mar	1822	78	S			
		Robert Kasey	Servant	B	M	May	1876	24	S			
36	36	Sally Wright	Head	W	F	Sep	1809	90	Wd	0		
		Henrietta Turner	Servant	B	F	Octo	1860	39	S			

Name of each person whose place of abode on June 1, 1900, was in this family. [continued from prior page]	Nativity — Place of birth of each person and parents of each person enumerated.			Citizenship			Occupation, Trade, Or Profession of each person Ten Years of age and over.		Education			
	Place of birth of this Person	Place of birth of Father of this person	Place of birth of Mother of this person	Year of immigration to the United States	Number of years in the United States	Natural-ization	Occupation	Months not employed	Attended school in months)	Can read	Can write	Can speak English
Cicero A. Wright	Virginia	Virginia	Virginia				Farmer	0		Yes	Yes	Yes
Gertrude Wright	Virginia	Virginia	Virginia							Yes	Yes	Yes
Mable C. Wright	Virginia	Virginia	Virginia									
Herbert M. Wright	Virginia	Virginia	Virginia									

Gills Creek District

Name	Place of birth of this Person	Place of birth of Father of this person	Place of birth of Mother of this person	Year of immigration	Number of years in US	Natural-ization	Occupation	Months not employed	Attended school in months	Can read	Can write	Can speak English
Nelly(?) L Starky	Virginia	Virginia	Virginia				Laundress	0		Yes	Yes	Yes
Robert I Starky	Virginia	Virginia	Virginia						0	No	No	Yes
Lucy J Starky	Virginia	Virginia	Virginia									
James H. Starky	Virginia	Virginia	Virginia									
Florence Wright	Virginia	Virginia	Virginia				Servant	0		No	No	Yes
John D Hannabas	Virginia	Virginia	Virginia				Farmer	0		Yes	Yes	Yes
Jammima(?) Hannabas	Virginia	Virginia	Virginia							Yes	Yes	Yes
Ola M Hannabas	Virginia	Virginia	Virginia						3	Yes	Yes	Yes
Fleming Wright	Virginia	Virginia	Virginia							Yes	Yes	Yes
Robert Kasey	Virginia	Virginia	Virginia				Farm Laborer	0		Yes	Yes	Yes
Sally Wright	Virginia	Virginia	Virginia							Yes	Yes	Yes
Henrietta Turner	Virginia	Virginia	Virginia				Servant			No	No	Yes

Appendix: Franklin County, Virginia, 1900 Census

<u>Ownership Of Home</u>

Name of each person whose place of abode on June 1, 1900, was in this family. [continued from prior page]	Owned or rented	Owned free or mortgaged	Farm or house	Number of farm schedule	Identification
Cicero A. Wright Gertrude Wright Mable C. Wright Herbert M. Wright	O	F	F	24	1919 Cicero A. Wright of Franklin County, son of 1890 Robert Penn Wright of Franklin County, grandson of 1849 Thomas Wright of Franklin County, great grandson of 1815 Joseph Wright of Bedford County and great grandson of 1803 John Wright of Bedford County, and great great grandson of 1763 Thomas Wright of Bedford County

<u>Gills Creek District</u>

Name	Owned or rented	Owned free or mortgaged	Farm or house	Number of farm schedule	Identification
Nelly(?) L Starky Robert I Starky Lucy J Starky James H. Starky Florence Wright	R		H		
John D Hannabas Jammima(?) Hannabas Ola M Hannabas Fleming Wright Robert Kasey	O	F	F	25	1901 Fleming J. T. Wright of Franklin County, son of 1855 Wright Wright of Franklin County, grandson of 1815 Joseph Wright of Franklin County, and great grandson of 1763 Thomas Wright of Franklin County
Sally Wright Henrietta Turner	R		H		Sarah R. E. (Jordan) Wright, widow of Joseph Kemp Wright, a son of 1855 Wright Wright of Franklin County, grandson of 1815 Joseph Wright of Bedford County, and great grandson of 1763 Thomas Wright of Bedford County

| | Location | | | | Relation | | | | Personal Description | | | | | | |

Street	House Number	Number of dwelling houses in the order of visitation	Number of family in the order of visitation	Name of each person whose place of abode on June 1, 1900, was in this family.	Relation-ship of each person to the head the family	Color or race	Sex	Date of Birth Month	Year	Age at last birth-day	Whether single, married, widowed, or divorced	Number of years married	Mother of how many children	Number of these children living
		148	152	Laurence Wright	Head	W	M	Aug	1847	52	Wd			
				Della R. Wright	Daughter	W	F	July	1872	27	D		1	1
				Eugene E Wright	Son	W	M	Apr	1885	15	S			
				Guthrie Webb	Gson	W	M	Feb	1894	6	S			
		149	153	Peter Meador	Head	B	M	July	1870	29	M	10		
				Arbella Meador	Wife	B	F	Mar	1880	20	M	10	4	3
				Amon H Meador	Son	B	M	Mar	1893	7	S			
				Laura N Meador	Daughter	B	F	Aug	1894	5	S			
				Margarette Meador	Daughter	B	F	July	1899	10/12	S			
				Pleas Wright	Servant	B	M	Feb	1885	15	S			
		150	154	Lucy Wright	Head	B	F	Mar	1855	45	S		3	3
				Callie Wright	Daughter	B	F	Apr	1888	12	S			
		346	350	Robert W(?) Wright	Head	B	M	Feb	1867	33	M	10		
				Hattie L. Wright	Wife	B	F	Aug	1873	26	M	10	4	3
				Horace L. Wright	Son	B	M	Mar	1892	8	S			
				Lollie K. Wright	Daughter	B	F	Apr	1896	4	S			
				Pauline C. Wright	Daughter	B	F	Jany	1899	1	S			
				Isaac St. Clair	F-in-law	B	M	Feb	1830	70	M	38		
				Margaret E St. Clair	M-in-law	B	F	Mar	1840	60	M	38	11	8
				Sylvester M. St. Clair	Nephew	B	M	Apr	1892	8	S			
				Harry L. St. Clair	Nephew	B	M	Sep	1894	5	S			
				Basset St. Clair	B-in-law	B	M	Jay	1875	25	S			

Appendix: Franklin County, Virginia, 1900 Census

| Name of each person whose place of abode on June 1, 1900, was in this family. [continued from prior page] | Nativity | | | Citizenship | | | Occupation, Trade, Or Profession of each person Ten Years of age and over. | | Education | | | |
| | Place of birth of each person and parents of each person enumerated. | | | | | | | | | | | |
	Place of birth of this Person	Place of birth of Father of this person	Place of birth of Mother of this person	Year of immi-gration to the United States	Number of years in the United States	Natural-ization	Occupation	Months not employed	Attended school in months)	Can read	Can write	Can speak English
Laurence Wright	Virginia	Virginia	Virginia				Farmer	0		Yes	Yes	Yes
Della R. Wright	Virginia	Virginia	Virginia							Yes	Yes	Yes
Eugene E Wright	Virginia	Virginia	Virginia				Farm Laborer	0		Yes	Yes	Yes
Guthrie Webb	Virginia	Virginia	Virginia						5	Yes	Yes	Yes
Peter Meador	Virginia	Virginia	Virginia				Farmer	0		No	No	Yes
Arbella Meador	Virginia	Virginia	Virginia							Yes	Yes	Yes
Amon H Meador	Virginia	Virginia	Virginia						0	No	No	No
Laura N Meador	Virginia	Virginia	Virginia						0	No	No	Yes
Margarette Meador	Virginia	Virginia	Virginia									
Pleas Wright	Virginia	Virginia	Virginia				Farm Laborer	0	0	No	No	Yes
Lucy Wright	Virginia	Virginia	Virginia				Laundress	0	0	No	No	Yes
Callie Wright	Virginia	Virginia	Virginia							No	No	Yes
Robert Wright	Virginia	Virginia	Virginia				Blacksmith	0		Yes	Yes	Yes
Hattie L. Wright	Virginia	Virginia	Virginia							Yes	Yes	Yes
Horace L. Wright	Virginia	Virginia	Virginia						0	No	No	Yes
Lollie K. Wright	Virginia	Virginia	Virginia									
Pauline C. Wright	Virginia	Virginia	Virginia									
Isaac St. Clair	Virginia	Virginia	Virginia							No	No	No
Margaret E St. Clair	Virginia	Virginia	Virginia							No	No	Yes
Sylvester M. St. Clair	Virginia	Virginia	Virginia						0	No	No	Yes
Harry L. St. Clair	Virginia	Virginia	Virginia						0	No	No	Yes
Basset St. Clair	Virginia	Virginia	Virginia				Day Laborer	6		Yes	Yes	Yes

Appendix: Franklin County, Virginia, 1900 Census

<u>_____ Ownership Of Home _____</u>

Name of each person whose place of abode on June 1, 1900, was in this family. [continued from prior page]	Owned or rented	Owned free or mortgaged	Farm or house	Number of farm schedule	Identification
Laurence Wright Della R. Wright Eugene E Wright Guthrie Webb		F	F	117	1933 Laurence Monroe Wright of Franklin County, son of 1890 Robert Penn Wright of Franklin County, grandson of 1849 Thomas Wright of Franklin County, great grandson of 1815 Joseph Wright of Bedford County and great grandson of 1803 John Wright of Bedford County, and great great grandson of 1763 Thomas Wright of Bedford County
Peter Meador Arbella Meador Amon H Meador Laura N Meador Margarette Meador Pleas Wright	R		F	118	
Lucy Wright Callie Wright	R		H		
Robert Wright Hattie L. Wright Horace L. Wright Lollie K. Wright Pauline C. Wright Isaac St. Clair Margaret E St. Clair Sylvester M. St. Clair Harry L. St. Clair Basset St. Clair	O		H		Robert Wright, son of Pleasant Wright

Appendix: Franklin County, Virginia, 1900 Census

					Relation									
		Location						**Personal Description**						

In Cities Street	House Number	Number of dwelling houses in the order of visitation	Number of family in the order of visitation	Name of each person whose place of abode on June 1, 1900, was in this family.	Relation-ship of each person to the head the family	Color or race	Sex	Date of Birth Month	Year	Age at last birth-day	Whether single, married, widowed, or divorced	Number of years married	Mother of how many children	Number of these children living
		5	5	Samuel L. Wright	Head	W	M	Nov	1871	39/38	M	11		
				Sarah E. Wright	Wife	W	F	March	1875	25	M	11	4	4
				Willie M. Wright	Daughter	W	F	Jany	1890	10	S			
				James Wright	Son	W	M	April	1892	8	S			
				Lester R. Wright	Son	W	M	July	1893	6	S			
				Laura F. Wright	Daughter	W	F	March	1898	2	S			
		237	238	Ace H Newman	Head	W	M	May	1831	69	M	41		
				Lydia Newman	Wife	W	F	Jan	1842	58	M	41	10	8
				Sophia E Wright	Daughter	W	F	Dec	1879	20	M	8	5	4
				James H Wright	G son	W	M	July	1894	5	S			
				Thomas P Wright	G son	W	M	April	1896	4	S			
				Florence E Wright	G Daughter	W	F	Feb	1898	2	S			
				Lydia M Wright	G Daughter	W	F	March	1900	2/12	S			
				Irwin Fink	Servant	B	M	Sept	1882	18	S			

Little Creek District

In Cities Street	House Number	Number of dwelling houses in the order of visitation	Number of family in the order of visitation	Name of each person	Relationship	Color or race	Sex	Month	Year	Age	Status	Years married	Mother of how many children	Number living
		65	65	Joshua Wright	Head	B	M	May	1824	76	M	2		
				Martha Wright	Wife	B	F	May	1834	66	M	2	0	0
				Pat Childress	G son	B	M	Apr	1887	13	S			
		201	201	John W. Wright	Head	W	M	Aug	1873	26	M	3		
				Sarah C. Wright	Wife	W	F	Apr	1874	26	M	3	2	2
				James H. Wright	Son	W	M	Dec	1898	2	S			
				Myrtle Wright	Daughter	W	F	Mar	1900	2/12	S			

Appendix: Franklin County, Virginia, 1900 Census

Name of each person whose place of abode on June 1, 1900, was in this family. [continued from prior page]	Nativity			Citizenship			Occupation, Trade, Or Profession of each person Ten Years of age and over.		Education			
	Place of birth of this Person	Place of birth of Father of this person	Place of birth of Mother of this person	Year of immigration to the United States	Number of years in the United States	Naturalization	Occupation	Months not employed	Attended school in months)	Can read	Can write	Can speak English
Samuel L. Wright	Virginia	Virginia	Virginia				Day Laborer	0		No	No	Yes
Sarah E. Wright	North Carolina	Virginia	Virginia							No	No	Yes
Willie M. Wright	Virginia	Virginia	North Carolina						0	No	No	Yes
James Wright	Virginia	Virginia	North Carolina						0			
Lester R. Wright	Virginia	Virginia	North Carolina						0			
Laura F. Wright	Virginia	Virginia	North Carolina									
Ace H Newman	Virginia	Virginia	Virginia				Farmer	0		Yes	Yes	Yes
Lydia Newman	Virginia	Virginia	Virginia							Yes	Yes	Yes
Sophia E Wright	Virginia	Virginia	Virginia						0	Yes	Yes	Yes
James H Wright	Virginia	Virginia	Virginia						0			
Thomas P Wright	Virginia	Virginia	Virginia									
Florence E Wright	Virginia	Virginia	Virginia									
Lydia M Wright	Virginia	Virginia	Virginia									
Irwin Fink	Virginia	Virginia	Virginia				Farm laborer	0	2	Yes	No	Yes

Little Creek District

Joshua Wright	Virginia	Virginia	Virginia							No	No	Yes
Martha Wright	Virginia	Virginia	Virginia							No	No	Yes
Pat Childress	Virginia	Virginia	Virginia						0	No	No	Yes
John W. Wright	Virginia	Virginia	Virginia				Day Laborer			Yes	Yes	Yes
Sarah C. Wright	Virginia	Virginia	Virginia							Yes	Yes	Yes
James H. Wright	Virginia	Virginia	Virginia									
Myrtle Wright	Virginia	Virginia	Virginia									

Ownership Of Home

Name of each person whose place of abode on June 1, 1900, was in this family. [continued from prior page]	Owned or rented	Owned free or mortgaged	Farm or house	Number of farm schedule	Identification
Samuel L. Wright	R		H		
Sarah E. Wright					
Willie M. Wright					
James Wright					
Lester R. Wright					
Laura F. Wright					
Ace H Newman	O	M	F	203	Sophia L. B. (Newman) Wright, wife of James B. Wright, a son of Loving A. Wright, grandson of 1854 Samuel A. Wright of Appomattox County, great grandson of 1820 Pryor Wright, Sr., of Prince Edward County, and great great grandson of 1779 John Wright of Prince Edward County
Lydia Newman					
Sophia E Wright					
James H Wright					
Thomas P Wright					
Florence E Wright					
Lydia M Wright					
Irwin Fink					

Little Creek District

Joshua Wright	O	F	H		
Martha Wright					
Pat Childress					
John W. Wright	O	M	H		John W. Wright, son of Abraham H. Wright, grandson of 1896 John B. Wright of Franklin County, great grandson of 1823 James Wright of Franklin County, great great grandson of 1809 William Wright of Franklin County, and probably great great great grandson of 1792 John Wright of Fauquier County
Sarah C. Wright					
James H. Wright					
Myrtle Wright					

Location					Relation		Personal Description								
In Cities		Number of dwelling houses in the order of visitation	Number of family in the order of visitation	Name of each person whose place of abode on June 1, 1900, was in this family.	Relationship of each person to the head the family	Color or race	Sex	Date of Birth Month	Year	Age at last birthday	Whether single, married, widowed, or divorced	Number of years married	Mother of how many children	Number of these children living
Street	House Number													
		209	209	James G Wright	Head	W	M	Aug	1832	67	M	7		
				Arena(?) Wright	Wife	W	F	Oct	1853	46	M	7	0	0
		250	250	James W. Wright	Head	W	M	Mar	1855	45	M	20		
				Mary A. Wright	Wife	W	F	May	1850	50	M	20	2	2
				Josie Wright	Daughter	W	F	Feb	1884	16				
				Charlie Wright	Son	W	M	Mar	1883	17				
		260	260	John A(?) Wright	Head	W	M	Apr	1818	87	M	48		
				Mary Wright	Wife	W	F	Apr	1829	71	M	48	2	1
				Sally Pearson	Sister-in-law	W	F	Aug	1831	68	S			
				Johnnie M Wright	G Daughter	W	F	Jan	1892	7	S			

Appendix: Franklin County, Virginia, 1900 Census

Name of each person whose place of abode on June 1, 1900, was in this family. [continued from prior page]	Nativity			Citizenship			Occupation, Trade, Or Profession of each person Ten Years of age and over.		Education		
	Place of birth of this Person	Place of birth of Father of this person	Place of birth of Mother of this person	Year of immigration to the United States	Number of years in the United States	Natural-ization	Occupation	Months not employed	Attended school in months)	Can read	Can write	Can speak English
James G Wright	Virginia	Virginia	Virginia				Farmer	0		Yes	Yes	Yes
Arena(?) Wright	Virginia	Virginia	Virginia							Yes	Yes	Yes
James W. Wright	Virginia	Virginia	Virginia				Farm laborer	1		Yes	Yes	Yes
Mary A. Wright	Virginia	Virginia	Virginia							Yes	Yes	Yes
Josie Wright	Virginia	Virginia	Virginia						0	Yes	Yes	Yes
Charlie Wright	Virginia	Virginia	Virginia				At school		4	Yes	Yes	Yes
John A(?) Wright	Virginia	Virginia	Virginia				Farmer	0		Yes	Yes	Yes
Mary Wright	Virginia	Virginia	Virginia							Yes	Yes	Yes
Sally Pearson	Virginia	Virginia	Virginia				House Keeper	0				
Johnnie M Wright	Virginia	Virginia	Virginia									

Appendix: Franklin County, Virginia, 1900 Census

<u>Ownership Of Home</u>

Name of each person whose place of abode on June 1, 1900, was in this family. [continued from prior page]	Owned or rented	Owned free or mortgaged	Farm or house	Number of farm schedule	Identification
James G Wright Arena(?) Wright	O	F	F	186	1905 James G. Wright of Franklin County, son of 1896 John B. Wright of Franklin County, grandson of 1823 James Wright of Franklin County, great grandson of 1809 William Wright of Franklin County, and probably great great grandson of 1792 John Wright of Fauquier County
James W. Wright Mary A. Wright Josie Wright Charlie Wright	O	M	H		James W. T. Wright, son of James G. Wright, Jr., grandson of James Grant Wright, great grandson of 1823 James Wright of Franklin County, great great grandson of 1809 William Wright of Franklin County, and probably great great great grandson of 1792 John Wright of Fauquier County
John W Wright Mary Wright Sally Pearson Johnnie M Wright	O	F	F	185	1905 John A. Wright of Franklin County, son of 1843 George Wright of Franklin County and grandson of 1809 William Wright of Franklin County, and probably great grandson of 1792 John Wright of Fauquier County

Appendix: Franklin County, Virginia, 1900 Census

Location				Relation			Personal Description						

In Cities		Number of dwelling houses in the order of visitation	Number of family in the order of visitation	Name of each person whose place of abode on June 1, 1900, was in this family.	Relation-ship of each person to the head the family	Color or race	Sex	Date of Birth		Age at last birth-day	Whether single, married, widowed, or divorced	Number of years married	Mother of how many children	Number of these children living
Street	House Number							Month	Year					

Long Branch District

		60	60	John W Wright	Head	W	M	July	1852	47	M	22		
				Nancy J. Wright	Wife	W	F	Jan	1859	41	M	22	11	10
				Girley R. Wright	Daughter	W	F	Apr	1881	19	S			
				Salley B. Wright	Daughter	W	F	Oct	1883	16	S			
				John H. Wright	Son	W	M	Mar	1885	15	S			
				James R. Wright	Son	W	M	Apr	1887	13	S			
				Margrat S. Wright	Daughter	W	F	Mar	1890	10	S			
				Piliot M. J. Wright	Son	W	M	June	1892	7	S			
				George W. Wright	Son	W	M	Nov	1893	6	S			
				Elizie J. Wright	Son	W	M	Oct	1896	3	S			
				Mary L Wright	Daughter	W	F	Apr	1900	1/12	S			
				Martha A Wright	Sister	W	F	July	1849	51	S			

Magodee District

		67	67	Charles Wright	Head	W	M	Dec	1874	25	M	1		
				Mary E. Wright	Wife	W	F	Aug	1873	26	M	1	1	1
				Annie M. Wright	Daughter	W	F	Apr	1900	1/12	S			

Appendix: Franklin County, Virginia, 1900 Census

Name of each person whose place of abode on June 1, 1900, was in this family. [continued from prior page]	Nativity			Citizenship			Occupation, Trade, Or Profession of each person Ten Years of age and over.		Education			
	Place of birth of this Person	Place of birth of Father of this person	Place of birth of Mother of this person	Year of immigration to the United States	Number of years in the United States	Naturalization	Occupation	Months not employed	Attended school in months)	Can read	Can write	Can speak English
Long Branch District												
John W Wright	Virginia	Virginia	Virginia				Farmer	6		No	No	Yes
Nancy J. Wright	Virginia	Virginia	Virginia							No	No	Yes
Girley R. Wright	Virginia	Virginia	Virginia						0	No	No	Yes
Salley B. Wright	Virginia	Virginia	Virginia						0	No	No	Yes
John H. Wright	Virginia	Virginia	Virginia				Farm Labor	0	0	No	No	Yes
James R. Wright	Virginia	Virginia	Virginia				Farm Labor	0	0	No	No	Yes
Margrat S. Wright	Virginia	Virginia	Virginia						0	No	No	Yes
Piliot M. J. Wright	Virginia	Virginia	Virginia						0			
George W. Wright	Virginia	Virginia	Virginia						0			
Elizie J. Wright	Virginia	Virginia	Virginia									
Nancy Wright	Virginia	Virginia	Virginia									
Martha Wright	Virginia	Virginia	Virginia				House Keeper			No	No	Yes
Magodee District												
Charles Wright	Virginia	Virginia	Virginia				Farmer	0		Yes	Yes	Yes
Mary E. Wright	Virginia	Virginia	Virginia							Yes	Yes	Yes
Annie M. Wright	Virginia	Virginia	Virginia									

Ownership Of Home

Name of each person whose place of abode on June 1, 1900, was in this family. [continued from prior page]	Owned or rented	Owned free or mortgaged	Farm or house	Number of farm schedule	Identification
Long Branch District					
John W Wright	R		F	60	
Nancy J. Wright					
Girley R. Wright					
Salley B. Wright					
John H. Wright					
James R. Wright					
Margrat S. Wright					
Piliot M. J. Wright					
George W. Wright					
Elizie J. Wright					
Nancy Wright					
Martha Wright					
Magodee District					
Charles Wright	R		F	55	Charles A. Wright, son of Abraham H. Wright, grandson of 1896 John B. Wright of Franklin County, great grandson of 1823 James Wright of Franklin County, great great grandson of 1809 William Wright of Franklin County, and probably great great great grandson of 1792 John Wright of Fauquier County
Mary E. Wright					
Annie M. Wright					

	Location				Relation			Personal Description						
	In Cities	Number of dwelling houses in	Number of family in the	Name of each person whose place of	Relation-ship of each person					Age at last birth-	Whether single, married, widowed,	Number of years	Mother of how many	Number of these children
Street	House Number	the order of visitation	order of visitation	abode on June 1, 1900, was in this family.	to the head the family	Color or race	Sex	Date of Birth Month Year		day	or divorced	married	children	living
		195	195	George Wright	Head	W	M	Sept	1849	50	M	28		
				Callie Wright	Wife	W	F	May	1853	47	M	28	6	5
				Laura J. Gutherie	Daughter	W	F	Aprl	1881	19	M	0	1	1
				Isaac S. Wright	Son	W	M	May	1892	8	S			
				Lauvenia J. Wright	G Daughter	W	F	Aug	1889	10	S			
				Kent A. Gutherie	G son	W	M	May	1900	1/12	S			
				Robert L. Gutherie	Son-in-law	W	M	May	1873	27	M	0		
		196	196	Abraham H. Wright	Head	W	M	Oct	1834	65	M	28		
				Nancy A. Wright	Wife	W	F	May	1850	50	M	28	8	5
				Thomas J. Wright	Son	W	M	June	1879	20	S			
				Minnie Wright	Daughter	W	F	June	1885	15	S			

Rocky Mount District

		31	33	Colonel W Mills	Head	W	M	May	1864	36	M	8		
				Missouri F Mills	Wife	W	F	Oct	1863	36	M	8	3	2
				Walter F Mills	Son	W	M	June	1893	6	S			
				Piten Mills	son	W	M	Sept	1898	2	S			
				Gracie T Wright	Sister	W	F	Apr	1879	21	S			
		69	77	Sey(?) Mosley	Head	B	M	Feb	1863	27	M	2		
				Lucy Holland	Wife	W	F	Jan	1880	20	M	2	0	0
				Jane Wright	daughter	W	F	Mar	1884	16	S			
				William Jones	son	W	M	April	1881	19	S			
				Joel Angle(?)	boarder	W	M	March	1877	33	S			

| Name of each person whose place of abode on June 1, 1900, was in this family. [continued from prior page] | Nativity | | | Citizenship | | | Occupation, Trade, Or Profession of each person Ten Years of age and over. | | | Education | | |
| | Place of birth of each person and parents of each person enumerated. | | | | | | | | | | | |
	Place of birth of this Person	Place of birth of Father of this person	Place of birth of Mother of this person	Year of immi- gration to the United States	Number of years in the United States	Natural- ization	Occupation	Months not employed	Attended school in months)	Can read	Can write	Can speak English
George Wright	Virginia	Virginia	Virginia				Farmer	0		Yes	Yes	Yes
Callie Wright	Virginia	Virginia	Virginia							Yes	Yes	Yes
Laura J. Gutherie	Virginia	Virginia	Virginia				Housekeeper	0		Yes	Yes	Yes
Isaac S. Wright	Virginia	Virginia	Virginia				At school		5			
Lauvenia J. Wright	Virginia	Virginia	Virginia				At school		5	Yes	Yes	Yes
Kent A. Gutherie	Virginia	Virginia	Virginia									
Robert L. Gutherie	Virginia	Virginia	Virginia				Farm laborer	0		Yes	Yes	Yes
Abraham H. Wright	Virginia	Virginia	Virginia				Farmer	0		Yes	Yes	Yes
Nancy A. Wright	Virginia	Virginia	Virginia							No	No	Yes
Thomas J. Wright	Virginia	Virginia	Virginia				Day laborer	4		Yes	Yes	Yes
Minnie Wright	Virginia	Virginia	Virginia				At school		4	Yes	Yes	Yes

Rocky Mount District

Name	Place of birth of this Person	Place of birth of Father of this person	Place of birth of Mother of this person	Year of immi- gration	Number of years	Natural- ization	Occupation	Months not employed	Attended school in months)	Can read	Can write	Can speak English
Colonel W Mills	Virginia	Virginia	Virginia				Salesman	0		Yes	Yes	Yes
Missouri F Mills	Virginia	Virginia	Virginia							Yes	Yes	Yes
Walter F Mills	Virginia	Virginia	Virginia									
Piten Mills	Virginia	Virginia	Virginia									
Gracie T Wright	Virginia	Virginia	Virginia							Yes	Yes	Yes
Sey(?) Mosley	Virginia	Virginia	Virginia				Day laborer			No	No	Yes
Lucy Holland	Virginia	Virginia	Virginia				Washerwoman			No	No	Yes
Jane Wright	Virginia	Virginia	Virginia							No	No	Yes
William Jones	Virginia	Virginia	Virginia				Day laborer			No	No	Yes
Joel Angle(?)	Virginia	Virginia	Virginia				Sailer(?)			Yes	Yes	Yes

Appendix: Franklin County, Virginia, 1900 Census

Ownership Of Home

Name of each person whose place of abode on June 1, 1900, was in this family. [continued from prior page]	Owned or rented	Owned free or mortgaged	Farm or house	Number of farm schedule	Identification
George Wright Callie Wright Laura J. Gutherie Isaac S. Wright Lauvenia J. Wright Kent A. Gutherie Robert L. Gutherie	O	F	F	166	1923 George Greenberry Wright of Franklin County, son of 1896 John B. Wright of Franklin County, grandson of 1823 James Wright of Franklin County, great grandson of 1809 William Wright Wright of Franklin County, and probably great great grandson of 1792 John Wright of Fauquier County
Abraham H. Wright Nancy A. Wright Thomas J. Wright Minnie Wright	O	F	F	167	Abraham H. Wright, son of 1896 John B. Wright of Franklin County, grandson of 1823 James Wright of Franklin County, great grandson of 1809 William Wright Wright of Franklin County, and probably great great grandson of 1792 John Wright of Fauquier County

Rocky Mount District

Colonel W Mills Missouri F Mills Walter F Mills Piten Mills Gracie T Wright	R		H		Grace T. (Wright) Bussey, daughter of 1918 Otey Wright of Franklin County, granddaughter of 1839 John A. Wright of Franklin County, great granddaughter of 1830 William Wright of Franklin County, great great granddaughter of 1809 William Wright of Franklin County, and probably great great great granddaughter of 1792 John Wright of Fauquier County
Sey(?) Mosley Lucy Holland Jane Wright William Jones Joel Angle(?)			H		

	Location				Relation				Personal Description					
In Cities Street	House Number	Number of dwelling houses in the order of visitation	Number of family in the order of visitation	Name of each person whose place of abode on June 1, 1900, was in this family.	Relation-ship of each person to the head the family	Color or race	Sex	Date of Birth Month	Year	Age at last birth-day	Whether single, married, widowed, or divorced	Number of years married	Mother of how many children	Number of these children living
		235	248	Charles Wright	Head	B	M	Nov	1874	25	M	8		
				Sarah Wright	Wife	B	F	Nov	1874	26	M	8	4	4
				Lucy Wright	daughter	B	F	Apr	1893	7	S			
				Sallie Wright	daughter	B	F	Jun	1895	4	S			
				Hattie Wright	daughter	B	F	Nov	1897	3	S			
				Charlie Wright	son	B	M	June	1899	11/12	S			
				Andrew Bush	servant	B	M	May	1885	15	S			
		393	408	Jane C(?) Wright	Head	B	F	May	1870	30	M	11	3	3
				William Wright	son	B	M	Sep	1889	10	S			
				Rosa L. Wright	daughter	B	F	June	1892	7	S			
				Delbert F Wright	son	B	M	Dec	1894	5	S			
				Turner Mill	boarder	B	M	Jan	1870	30	S			
		128	136	Joseph Wright	Head	B	M	Mar	1855	45	M	16		
				Lula Wright	Wife	B	F	Oct	1859	40	M	16	5	5
				Elizabeth Wright	Daughter	B	F	May	1885	15	S			
				Minnie Wright	Daughter	B	F	Apr	1888	12	S			
				Lloyd Wright	Son	B	M	Dec	1891	8	S			
				Zela K. Wright	Daughter	B	F	Oct	1895	4	S			
				Clara Wright	Daughter	B	F	July	1897	2	S			

Name of each person whose place of abode on June 1, 1900, was in this family. [continued from prior page]	Nativity			Citizenship			Occupation, Trade, Or Profession of each person Ten Years of age and over.			Education		
	Place of birth of this Person	Place of birth of Father of this person	Place of birth of Mother of this person	Year of immi-gration to the United States	Number of years in the United States	Natural-ization	Occupation	Months not employed	Attended school in months)	Can read	Can write	Can speak English
Charles Wright	Virginia	Virginia	Virginia				Farmer	0		No	No	Yes
Sarah Wright	Virginia	Virginia	Virginia							Yes	Yes	Yes
Lucy Wright	Virginia	Virginia	Virginia						0			
Sallie Wright	Virginia	Virginia	Virginia									
Hattie Wright	Virginia	Virginia	Virginia									
Charlie Wright	Virginia	Virginia	Virginia									
Jane C(?) Wright	North Carolina	North Carolina	North Carolina							Yes	Yes	Yes
William Wright	North Carolina	North Carolina	North Carolina							Yes	No	Yes
Rosa L. Wright	North Carolina	North Carolina	North Carolina							Yes	No	Yes
Delbert F Wright	North Carolina	North Carolina	North Carolina									
Turner Mills	North Carolina	North Carolina	North Carolina				Minister	0		Yes	Yes	Yes
Joseph Wright	Virginia	Virginia	Virginia				Farmer	0		No	No	Yes
Lula Wright	Virginia	Virginia	Virginia							No	No	Yes
Elizabeth Wright	Virginia	Virginia	Virginia						5	Yes	No	Yes
Minnie Wright	Virginia	Virginia	Virginia						5	Yes	No	Yes
Lloyd Wright	Virginia	Virginia	Virginia						2	No	No	Yes
Zela K. Wright	Virginia	Virginia	Virginia							No	No	No
Clara Wright	Virginia	Virginia	Virginia									

Appendix: Franklin County, Virginia, 1900 Census

Ownership Of Home

Name of each person whose place of abode on June 1, 1900, was in this family. [continued from prior page]	Owned or rented	Owned free or mortgaged	Farm or house	Number of farm schedule	Identification
Charles Wright Sarah Wright Lucy Wright Sallie Wright Hattie Wright Charlie Wright	O	F	F	67	Charles Wright, son of Pleasant Wright
Jane C(?) Wright William Wright Rosa L. Wright Delbert F Wright Turner Mills	R		H		
Joseph Wright Lula Wright Elizabeth Wright Minnie Wright Lloyd Wright Zela K. Wright Clara Wright	R		F	132	Joseph Wright, son of Robert Wright

Appendix: Franklin County, Virginia, 1900 Census

	Location				Relation			Personal Description						
		Number of dwelling houses in	Number of family in the	Name of each person whose place of	Relation-ship of each person					Age at last	Whether single, married, widowed,	Number of years	Mother of how many	Number of these children
In Cities	House	the order of	order of	abode on June 1, 1900,	to the head	Color		Date of Birth		birth-	or			
Street	Number	visitation	visitation	was in this family.	the family	or race	Sex	Month	Year	day	divorced	married	children	living

Union Hall District

		168	170	W. J. Wright	Head	W	M	Jun	1860	40	M	14		
				Ada A. Wright	Wife	W	F	Aug	1865	34	M	14	9	8
				Una L. Wright	Dgtr	W	F	Jul	1887	12	S			
				Ina G. Wright	Dgtr	W	F	Aug	1888	11	S			
				Elmo S. Wright	Son	W	M	Dec	1889	10	S			
				Annie W. Wright	Dgtr	W	F	Sep	1891	8	S			
				Claud S. Wright	Son	W	M	Aug	1893	6	S			
				Henry J. Wright	Son	W	M	Mar	1895	5	S			
				Gladdis B. Wright	Son	W	F	June	1897	2	S			
				Chas Wm. Wright	Son	W	M	June	1899	11/12	S			
				W.G. Cundiff	Cousin	W	M	Sep	1876	23	S			
		197	199	T.P. Wright	Head	B	M	Dec	1869	30	M	6		
				Elvira Wright	Wife	B	F	Mar	1871	29	M	6	5	4
				Louis A Wright	Son	B	M	Dec	1895	4	S			
				Kennett Wright	Son	B	M	Aug	1897	2	S			
				Sarah Wright	Dgter	B	F	Dec	1898	1	S			
				Fanny K. Wright	Dgter	B	F	May	1900	0/12	S			

Appendix: Franklin County, Virginia, 1900 Census

Name of each person whose place of abode on June 1, 1900, was in this family. [continued from prior page]	Nativity			Citizenship			Occupation, Trade, Or Profession of each person Ten Years of age and over.			Education		
	Place of birth of each person and parents of each person enumerated.			Year of immi-gration to the United States	Number of years in the United States	Natural-ization		Months not employed	Attended school in months)	Can read	Can write	Can speak English
	Place of birth of this Person	Place of birth of Father of this person	Place of birth of Mother of this person				Occupation					

Union Hall District

W. J. Wright	Virginia	Virginia	Virginia				Farmer	0		no	no	yes
Ada A. Wright	Virginia	Virginia	Virginia							yes	yes	yes
Una L. Wright	Virginia	Virginia	Virginia				at School		4	yes	yes	yes
Ina G. Wright	Virginia	Virginia	Virginia				at School		4	yes	yes	yes
Elmo S. Wright	Virginia	Virginia	Virginia				Farm Laborer			yes	yes	yes
Annie W. Wright	Virginia	Virginia	Virginia				At School		4	yes	yes	yes
Claud S. Wright	Virginia	Virginia	Virginia									
Henry J. Wright	Virginia	Virginia	Virginia									
Gladdis B. Wright	Virginia	Virginia	Virginia									
Chas Wm. Wright	Virginia	Virginia	Virginia									
W.G. Cundiff	Virginia	Virginia	Virginia									
T.P. Wright	Virginia	Virginia	Virginia				Farmer	0		yes	yes	yes
Elvira Wright	Virginia	Virginia	Virginia							no	no	yes
Louis A Wright	Virginia	Virginia	Virginia									
Kennett Wright	Virginia	Virginia	Virginia									
Sarah Wright	Virginia	Virginia	Virginia									
Fanny K. Wright	Virginia	Virginia	Virginia									

Appendix: Franklin County, Virginia, 1900 Census

<u>Ownership Of Home</u>

Name of each person whose place of abode on June 1, 1900, was in this family. [continued from prior page]	Owned or rented	Owned free or mortgaged	Farm or house	Number of farm schedule	Identification
<u>Union Hall District</u>					
W. J. Wright	R		F	151	1920 Wilson J. Wright of Franklin County, son of 1862 Abraham O. Wright of Franklin County, grandson of 1883 Anslem Wright of Franklin County, and great grandson of William Wright
Ada A. Wright					
Una L. Wright					
Ina G. Wright					
Elmo S. Wright					
Annie W. Wright					
Claud S. Wright					
Henry J. Wright					
Gladdis B. Wright					
Chas Wm. Wright					
W.G. Cundiff					
T.P. Wright	R		F	178	
Elvira Wright					
Louis A Wright					
Kennett Wright					
Sarah Wright					
Fanny K. Wright					

	Location				Relation			Personal Description						
In Cities Street	House Number	Number of dwelling houses in the order of visitation	Number of family in the order of visitation	Name of each person whose place of abode on June 1, 1900, was in this family.	Relationship of each person to the head the family	Color or race	Sex	Month (Date of Birth)	Year	Age at last birthday	Whether single, married, widowed, or divorced	Number of years married	Mother of how many children	Number of these children living
		138	179	Jno W. Wright	Head	W	M	Nov	1854	45	M	19		
				Margaret Wright	Wife	W	F	Dec	1854	45	M	19	7	5
				Sallie M. Wright	Dgter	W	F	Nov	1882	17	S			
				Mary F. Wright	Dgter	W	F	Nov	1884	15	S			
				Lena P. Wright	Dgter	W	F	Aug	1885	14	S			
				Lulu A. Wright	Dgter	W	F	May	1888	12	S			
				Otie Wright	Son	W	M	Mar	1890	10	S			
		208	210	Lankford Wright	Head	B	M	May	1830	70	M	30		
				Lulu Wright	Wife	B	F	Sep	1839	60	M	30	4	3
				Susie Wright	GDter	B	F	May	1885	15	S			
		267	270	Joseph M Fralin	Head	W	M	May	1870	30	M	5		
				Wilmoth F. Fralin	Wife	W	F	Dec	1868	31	M	5	5	3
				Wm L. Fralin	Son	W	M	Sep	1895	4	S			
				Dewey George Frailin	Son	W	M	May	1897	3	S			
				Emma M Frailin	Dgter	W	F	Dec	1899	6/12	S			
				Elizabeth J. Wright	Mo-In-Law	W	F	May	1840	60	W	6	4	

Name of each person whose place of abode on June 1, 1900, was in this family. [continued from prior page]	Nativity			Citizenship			Occupation, Trade, Or Profession of each person Ten Years of age and over.		Education			
	Place of birth of each person and parents of each person enumerated.												
	Place of birth of this Person	Place of birth of Father of this person	Place of birth of Mother of this person	Year of immigration to the United States	Number of years in the United States	Natural-ization	Occupation	Months not employed	Attended school in months)	Can read	Can write	Can speak English
Jno W. Wright	Virginia	Virginia	Virginia				Farmer		0	No	Yes	Yes
Margaret Wright	Virginia	Virginia	Virginia							Yes	Yes	Yes
Sallie M. Wright	Virginia	Virginia	Virginia				At School		4	Yes	Yes	Yes
Mary F. Wright	Virginia	Virginia	Virginia				At School		4	Yes	Yes	Yes
Lena P. Wright	Virginia	Virginia	Virginia				Do		4	Yes	Yes	Yes
Lulu A. Wright	Virginia	Virginia	Virginia				Do		4	Yes	Yes	Yes
Otie Wright	Virginia	Virginia	Virginia							No	No	Yes
Lankford Wright	Virginia	Virginia	Virginia				Farm Laborer	0		No	No	Yes
Lulu Wright	Virginia	Virginia	Virginia							No	No	Yes
Susie Wright	Virginia	Virginia	Virginia							No	No	Yes
Joseph M Fralin	Virginia	Virginia	Virginia				Farmer		0	yes	yes	yes
Wilmoth F. Fralin	Virginia	Virginia	Virginia							yes	yes	yes
Wm L. Fralin	Virginia	Virginia	Virginia									
Dewey George Frailin	Virginia	Virginia	Virginia									
Emma M Frailin	Virginia	Virginia	Virginia									
Elizabeth J. Wright	Virginia	Virginia	Virginia				Housekeeper		0	yes	yes	yes

Ownership Of Home

Name of each person whose place of abode on June 1, 1900, was in this family. [continued from prior page]	Owned or rented	Owned free or mortgaged	Farm or house	Number of farm schedule	Identification
Jno W. Wright Margaret Wright Sallie M. Wright Mary F. Wright Lena P. Wright Lulu A. Wright Otie Wright	R		F	122	John W. Wright, son of 1862 Abraham O. Wright of Franklin County, grandson of 1883 Anslem Wright of Franklin County, and great grandson of William Wright
Lankford Wright Lulu Wright Susie Wright	O	M	F	189	Lankford Wright, son of Tandy Graves
Joseph M Fralin Wilmoth F. Fralin Wm L. Fralin Dewey George Frailin Emma M Frailin Elizabeth J. Wright	R		F	243	Eliza A. (Brown) Wright, widow of 1884 William R. Wright of Franklin County, a son of 1883 Anslem Wright of Franklin County and grandson of William Wright

Whitlow, Hastie, 92, 93
Whorley, Ayliss, 88, 89
Whorley, Samuel, 88, 89
Wingfield, George, 94, 95
Wright, A. Calla, 122, 123
Wright, Abraham, 60, 65
Wright, Abraham H., 166, 167, 168
Wright, Abram, 69, 122, 123
Wright, Abram O., 70
Wright, Ada, 90, 91
Wright, Ada A., 172, 173, 174
Wright, Aggy, 84, 85
Wright, Agness, 110, 111
Wright, Alean, 71
Wright, Alice, 122, 123
Wright, Alis C., 142, 143, 144
Wright, Allie, 136, 137, 138
Wright, Althea S., 128, 129
Wright, Amanda E., 120, 121
Wright, Ambrose, 14, 15, , 16,, 24, 25, 26, 27, 28, 29
Wright, Ammon, 62
Wright, Andrew, 60, 86, 87
Wright, Andrew J., 75, 120, 121
Wright, Ann, 64, 65
Wright, Annie M., 163, 164, 165
Wright, Annie W., 172, 173, 174
Wright, Ansalom, 60
Wright, Anslem, 120, 121
Wright, Ansolem, 30, 31, 32, 33, 34, 35, 38, 39, 40, 41, 42, 43, 44
Wright, Ansom, 70
Wright, Anthoney, 71
Wright, Anthony, 65
Wright, Arena(?), 160, 161, 162
Wright, Arkansas, 102, 103, 142, 143, 144
Wright, Asa, 63, 73, 80, 81, 106, 107, 145, 146, 147
Wright, Benjamin C, 142, 143, 144
Wright, Berta, 148, 149, 150
Wright, Bettie A., 102, 103

Wright, Bettie C., 108, 109
Wright, Birta, 142, 143, 144
Wright, Brad B., 139, 140, 141
Wright, Brir, 88, 89
Wright, Callie, 154, 155, 156, 166, 167, 168
Wright, Callie M., 148, 149, 150
Wright, Caroline, 128, 129
Wright, Caroline F., 73
Wright, Carrol W., 148, 149, 150
Wright, Catharine, 66, 148, 149, 150
Wright, Cathrine, 110, 111
Wright, Charles, 110, 111, 145, 146, 147, 163, 164, 165, 169, 170, 171
Wright, Charles C., 72
Wright, Charley, 122, 123,
Wright, Charlie, 160, 161, 162, 169, 170, 171
Wright, Charlotte, 60, 62,63, 88, 89, 124, 125
Wright, Chas, 128, 129
Wright, Chas Wm., 172, 173, 174
Wright, Chester A., 136, 137, 138
Wright, Cicero, 84, 85
Wright, Cicero A., 76, 151, 152, 153
Wright, Cisaroe A., 112, 113
Wright, Clara, 169, 170, 171
Wright, Clarry, 136, 137, 138
Wright, Claud S., 172, 173, 174
Wright, Cora L., 108, 109
Wright, Cordelia, 122, 123
Wright, Crockett, 102, 103, 142, 143, 144
Wright, Crockett A., 72
Wright, Cynthia, 62
Wright, Dalton C., 148, 149, 150
Wright, Dandrige, 128, 129
Wright, Dandrige A., 145, 146, 147
Wright, Dasie C., 139, 140, 141
Wright, David, 17, 18, 19, 72, 102, 103
Wright, Deborah J., 148, 149, 150
Wright, Delbert F, 169, 170, 171
Wright, Della R., 154, 155, 156

Wright, Dellah R., 118, 119
Wright, Dewie D., 139, 140, 141
Wright, E J, 130, 131
Wright, Edmund, 148, 149, 150
Wright, Elaine, 124, 125
Wright, Eldrige, 145, 146, 147
Wright, Eliza Ann, 120, 121
Wright, Eliza W., 120, 121
Wright, Elizabeth, 45, 46, 47, 48, 49, 50, 51, 62, 63, 64, 66, 68, 70, 72, 73, 77, 169, 170, 171
Wright, Elizabeth A., 102, 103, 136, 137, 138
Wright, Elizabeth J., 175, 176, 177
Wright, Elizie J., 163, 164, 165
Wright, Ellen, 100, 101, 124, 125
Wright, Elliott, 62
Wright, Elmo S., 172, 173, 174
Wright, Elvira, 172, 173, 174
Wright, Emlly, 96, 97, 126, 127
Wright, Emily E., 142, 143, 144
Wright, Emma, 126, 127
Wright, Enoch, 4, 5
Wright, Ethel C., 145, 146, 147
Wright, Eugene E, 154, 155, 156
Wright, Eva E., 148, 149, 150
Wright, Evvie G., 136, 137, 138
Wright, Ezekiel, 8, 9, 10, 30, 31, 32, 33, 34, 35, 38, 39, 40, 41, 42, 43, 44, 64, 68, 88, 89
Wright, F. J. T., 75, 118, 119
Wright, Fannie, 96, 97
Wright, Fanny, 145, 146, 147
Wright, Fanny K., 172, 173, 174
Wright, Ferdersie A., 142, 143, 144
Wright, Fleming, 151, 152, 153
Wright, Fleming J. T., 61
Wright, Fletcher, 84, 85,
Wright, Florence, 84, 85, 151, 152, 153
Wright, Florence E, 157, 158, 159
Wright, Frances, 94, 95, 112, 113

Wright, Frances E., 126, 127
Wright, Frank N., 145, 146, 147
Wright, G. G., 122, 123
Wright, Geneva, 139, 140, 141
Wright, Geo, 69
Wright, Geo F., 74
Wright, George, 2, 3, 8, 9, 10, 11, 12, 13, 20, 21, 22, 24, 25, 26, 27, 28, 29, 38, 39, 40, 41, 42, 43, 44, 62, 63, 65, 80, 81, 90, 91, 92, 93, 166, 167, 168
Wright, George A, 45, 46, 47, 48, 49, 50, 51, 102, 103, 136, 137, 138
Wright, George C., 60
Wright, George F, 45, 46, 47, 48, 49, 50, 51, 62
Wright, George Finay, 24, 25, 26, 27, 28, 29
Wright, George H, 100, 101
Wright, George L, 38, 39, 40, 41, 42, 43, 44
Wright, George O., 145, 146, 147
Wright, George T, 102, 103
Wright, George W, 45, 46, 47, 48, 49, 50, 51, 62, 163, 164, 165
Wright, Gertrude, 151, 152, 153
Wright, Girley R., 163, 164, 165
Wright, Gladdis B., 172, 173, 174
Wright, Goodman A., 66
Wright, Gracie T, 166, 167, 168
Wright, Green, 110, 111, 118, 119
Wright, Grief, 14, 15, 16
Wright, Gustavus, 145, 146, 147
Wright, Harriet A., 142, 143, 144
Wright, Harriett, 72
Wright, Harris, 136, 137, 138
Wright, Hattie, 169, 170, 171
Wright, Hattie L., 154, 155, 156
Wright, Henrietta, 84, 85, 148, 149, 150
Wright, Henry, 84, 85
Wright, Henry C., 104, 105, 139, 140, 141
Wright, Henry J., 172, 173, 174
Wright, Henry S., 75, 76, 104, 105, 118, 119
Wright, Herbert M., 151, 152, 153
Wright, Hiram, 11, 12, 13
Wright, Horace L., 154, 155, 156

Wright, Larance M., 76
Wright, Laticia, 92, 93
Wright, Latitia, 100, 101
Wright, Laura F., 157, 158, 159
Wright, Laurence, 154, 155, 156
Wright, Laurence M., 61, 118, 119
Wright, Lauvenia J., 166, 167, 168
Wright, Lawrence, 84, 85
Wright, Leaoky, 112, 113
Wright, Lena P., 175, 176, 177
Wright, Lester R., 157, 158, 159
Wright, Letitia, 60
Wright, Lewis, 110, 111
Wright, Lloyd, 169, 170, 171
Wright, Lollie K., 154, 155, 156
Wright, Longfoot, 96, 97
Wright, Louis A, 172, 173, 174
Wright, Louisa, 60, 70, 94, 95, 112, 113
Wright, Louretta C., 120, 121
Wright, Lucinda, 145, 146, 147
Wright, Lucy, 154, 155, 156, 169, 170, 171
Wright, Lucy E., 104, 105, 139, 140, 141
Wright, Lula, 169, 170, 171
Wright, Lulu, 175, 176, 177
Wright, Lulu A., 175, 176, 177
Wright, Lydia M, 157, 158, 159
Wright, Mable C., 151, 152, 153
Wright, Manassa, 84, 85, 110, 111
Wright, Margaret, 38, 39, 40, 41, 42, 43, 44, 65, 120, 121, 130, 131, 175, 176, 177
Wright, Margrat S., 163, 164, 165
Wright, Margt, 68
Wright, Maria, 84, 85, 128, 129
Wright, Mariah, 110, 111
Wright, Mark, 90, 91
Wright, Martha, 86, 87, 122, 123, 157, 158, 159, 164, 165
Wright, Martha A, 163
Wright, Martha F, 139, 140, 141

Wright, Martin, 20, 21, 22
Wright, Mary, 60, 61, 63, 64, 65, 68, 69, 73, 75, 77, 80, 81, 92, 93, 124, 125, 160, 161, 162
Wright, Mary A., 61, 75, 118, 119, 160, 161, 162
Wright, Mary E., 60, 102, 72, 73, 103, 130, 131, 136, 137, 138, 163, 164, 165
Wright, Mary F., 126, 127, 175, 176, 177
Wright, Mary L., 104, 105, 163
Wright, McGeorge M., 148, 149, 150
Wright, Millie, 92, 93, 100, 101
Wright, Milton, 84, 85
Wright, Milton M, 76, 112, 113
Wright, Minnie, 124, 125, 142, 143, 144, 166, 167, 168, 169, 170, 171
Wright, Misura, 128, 129
Wright, Mollie, 142, 143, 144
Wright, Monldee E., 139, 140, 141
Wright, Moses, 11, 12, 13
Wright, Myrtle, 157, 158, 159
Wright, Nancy, 24, 25, 26, 27, 28, 29, 65, 74, 80, 81, 84, 85, 122, 123, 104, 165
Wright, Nancy A., 166, 167, 168
Wright, Nancy E., 102, 103, 142, 143, 144
Wright, Nancy J., 118, 119, 163, 164, 165
Wright, Nancy L., 76, 112, 113
Wright, Nannie, 126, 127
Wright, Nanny, 96, 97
Wright, Noah S., 142, 143, 144
Wright, O. R. F. H., 71
Wright, Oatey, 90, 91
Wright, Obadiah, 86, 87
Wright, Octava M, 148, 149, 150
Wright, Octavia, 84, 85
Wright, Octavia M., 114, 115
Wright, Olaver, 4, 5
Wright, Oliver, 60
Wright, Oliver J., 120, 121
Wright, Oliver T., 70
Wright, Olivia W., 136, 137, 138

Other Heritage Books by Robert N. Grant

Identifying the Wrights in the Goochland County, Virginia Tithe Lists, 1732-84

The Identification of 1809 William Wright of Franklin County, Virginia, as the Son of 1792 John Wright of Fauquier County, Virginia, and Elizabeth (Bronaugh) (Darnall) Wright

Wright Family Birth Records (1853-1896) and Marriage Records (1788-1915): Franklin County, Virginia, 1853-1896

Wright Family Birth Records, 1853-1896; Marriage Records, 1761-1900; Census Records, 1810-1900 in Amherst County, Virginia

Wright Family Birth Records (1853-1896) and Marriage Records (1782-1900): Campbell County, Virginia

Wright Family Birth Records, Marriage Records, and Personal Property Tax Lists: Appomattox County, Virginia

Wright Family Census Records, Deed Records, Land Tax Lists, Death Records and Probate Records: Appomattox County, Virginia

Wright Family Census Records: Bedford County, Virginia, 1810-1900

Wright Family Census Records: Campbell County, Virginia, 1810-1900

Wright Family Census Records: Franklin County, Virginia, 1810-1900

Wright Family Death Records (1853-1920), Cemetery Records by Cemetery, and Probate Records (1782-1900): Campbell County, Virginia

Wright Family Death Records (1854-1920), Cemetery Records by Cemetery, and Probate Records (1785-1928): Franklin County, Virginia

Wright Family Death, Cemetery and Probate Records: Bedford County, Virginia

Wright Family Deed Records (1782-1900) and Land Tax List (1782-1850): Campbell County, Virginia

Wright Family Land Grants (1785-1900) and Deed Records (1785-1897): Franklin County, Virginia

Wright Family Land Grants, Deed Records, Land Tax List, Death Records, Probate Records: Prince Edward County, Virginia

Wright Family Land Records: Bedford County, Virginia

Wright Family Land Tax Lists: Franklin County, Virginia, 1786-1860

Wright Family Land Tax Records: Amherst County, Virginia, 1782-1850

Wright Family Personal Property Tax Lists: Amherst County, Virginia, 1782-1850

Wright Family Personal Property Tax Lists: Campbell County, Virginia, 1785-1850

Wright Family Personal Property Tax Lists: Franklin County, Virginia, 1786-1850

Wright Family Personal Property Tax Records for Bedford County, Virginia, 1782 to 1850

Wright Family Records: Births in Bedford County, Virginia

Wright Family Records: Land Tax List, Bedford County, Virginia, 1782-1850

Wright Family Records: Lynchburg, Virginia Birth Records (1853-1896), Marriage Records (1805-1900), Marriage Notices (1794-1880), Census Records (1900), Deed Records (1805-1900), Death Records (1853-1896), Probate Records (1805-1900)

Wright Family Records: Marriages in Bedford County, Virginia

Wright Family Records: Prince Edward County, Virginia Birth Records, Marriage Records, Election Polls, and Tithe List, Personal Property Tax List, Census

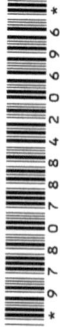